**Deepanjan Dey** is a senior HR leader and thought leader with over 28 years of experience across reputed manufacturing organizations. His career spans various sectors, including print media, petrochemicals, FMCG, refractories, cement and steel. He has deep expertise in employment law, industrial and employee relations, people processes, and talent management.

Author of *Contract Labour*, Deepanjan is also a regular contributor to leading HR journals and professional forums, writing on labour laws, workplace dynamics and contemporary HR challenges. He frequently engages with academic institutions and industry platforms, sharing practical insights drawn from decades of frontline leadership experience.

He was awarded the Future CHRO Award (2024) by CXO Lanes for his contributions to the HR profession.

You can connect with him on:
LinkedIn: www.linkedin.com/in/deepanjan-dey-1254b9155

# THE PERFECT INTERVIEW PLAYBOOK

How to Write Resumes, Prepare, Perform, and Win Jobs

DEEPANJAN DEY

Published by
Rupa Publications India Pvt. Ltd 2026
161-B/4, Gulmohar House,
Yusuf Sarai Community Centre,
New Delhi 110049

*Sales Centres:*
Bengaluru Chennai
Hyderabad Kolkata Mumbai



The views and opinions expressed in this book are the author's own and the facts are as reported by him; these have been verified to the extent possible, and the publishers are not in any way liable for the same.



P-ISBN: 978-93-7646-723-5
E-ISBN: 978-93-7646-222-3

First impression 2026

10 9 8 7 6 5 4 3 2 1



Printed in India

# Contents

# Prologue

Over the years, I have interviewed a number of candidates, and one thing has stood out—the majority are unprepared and haven't given enough thought to how they present themselves. Similarly, during my interactions with MBA students, I've observed a significant gap in guidance on preparing for and excelling in interviews. This realization inspired me to write this book, aimed at helping students, experienced professionals and anyone seeking to navigate the corporate world confidently.

Now, you might wonder—there are already numerous books on cracking interviews. What makes this one different?

This book is rooted in my personal journey, both as an interviewer and as an interviewee. Having a success rate of over 80 per cent in interviews I've attended, I believe there's value in sharing what has worked for me. Let me clarify—I wasn't a top-ranking student, nor do I hold degrees from elite institutions. Like many of you, I've faced my share of weaknesses and challenges. Yet, I've consistently managed to stand out and secure opportunities.

The secret lies in how you present yourself—your ability to 'sell' your strengths and create a lasting impression during the brief window of an interview. It's not just about answering questions; it's about showcasing your unique qualities, demonstrating confidence and leaving a mark that sets you apart.

This book will take you through the nuances of acing interviews, from preparation to performance. It's designed to help you build the confidence and skills needed to approach every interview with clarity and poise.

Whether you're a fresher stepping into the corporate world or a seasoned professional aiming for the next big role, I hope these pages equip you to transform interviews into stepping stones for your success.

Happy reading, and may you shine brightly in every interview you choose to take on!

## Part A

# LAYING THE FOUNDATION

# 1

# Your Resume: A Living Showcase of Your Potential

In cricket, matches aren't always won on the field—they're often decided on the pitch. A spinner may dominate in Chennai, a fast bowler in Perth, and sometimes, a poorly prepared surface may even result in match cancellation. The pitch doesn't just influence how the game is played—it decides if it will be played at all.

Your resume is that pitch.

It determines:

- Whether your interview will happen at all
- What kind of questions you'll face
- Whether you'll control the game—or defend throughout

Yet many candidates treat their resume like a static scoreboard. But it is not a summary of past scores—it's the pitch you prepare before your next innings. You may not control who interviews you or what they ask—but your resume can guide them toward your strengths.

**Why You Must Treat Your Resume like a Living Pitch**

- It sets the first impression—before you say a word.
- It decides if you will even get to play (shortlisting stage).
- It steers the interview—toward strengths or vulnerabilities.
- It reflects your preparedness, attention to detail and strategic thinking.

And like a pitch that changes session to session, your resume must evolve—not just when you change jobs, but with every new project, milestone or opportunity.

## RESUME PREPARATION: THE 7-LAYER PITCH

### 1. Lay a Flat, Readable Surface—Be Crisp and Clear

The tentative amount of time a recruiter gives to a particular CV before moving on to another is six to eight seconds. So, to create impact it needs to be crisp and clear. If it's dense, cluttered or vague—you're already out.

***Length Rule:***

- **Fresher:** one page
- **Mid-level:** two pages
- **Senior:** two to three pages (only relevant info)

***Do:***

- Use clean fonts (Calibri, Arial, size 10–12)
- Structured bullet points
- Clean sectioning: Summary | Experience | Education | Certifications | Skills

## 2. Read the Pitch Report—Tailor to the JD

A common mistake? Sending the same resume for every role.

That's like playing the same shots on a green-top and a turning track.

Each job description (JD) is a different pitch—and your resume must adapt to it.

**Let's Understand with Examples**

***Suppose you are an HR manager:***

**JD 1: Focus on Statutory Compliance and Labour Law**

'Looking for an HR professional with deep understanding of Factories Act, CLRA and experience in statutory audits.'

**Tailored Resume Bullet:**

'*Led monthly compliance reviews across three manufacturing sites; achieved 100 per cent statutory adherence under CLRA, Factories Act and ESI for two consecutive years.*'

**JD 2: Focus on Employee Engagement and Culture**

'We seek an HR professional to drive culture-building initiatives and employee retention programmes.'

**Tailored Resume Bullet:**

'*Designed and rolled out a value-driven engagement calendar, increasing employee satisfaction scores from 68 per cent to 84 per cent in 12 months.*'

**Now, let's assume you work in IT, sales or marketing.**

***Sales Executive***

**JD for Channel Sales**

'Build rural retail penetration across tier-3 cities.'

*'Expanded Kirana outreach from 85 to 240 outlets in four months; implemented visibility drives across two districts.'*

**JD for Institutional Sales**

'Manage large B2B accounts and contracts.'

*'Closed 14 institutional clients including hospitals and colleges; delivered 2.2 crore revenue in FY.'*

***Marketing Fresher***

**JD for Social Media Intern**

'Assist in increasing engagement and follower count.'

*'Developed Insta content strategy during internship; increased follower base by 3,000+ in two months.'*

**JD for Product Marketing Analyst**

'Assist in competitive benchmarking and Go To Market (GTM) planning.'

*'Conducted competitor feature matrix and pricing research for new launch; helped shape positioning strategy.'*

***Key Principle:***

Your resume must talk directly to the job description. Tailor the bullets. Use the JD's language. Show you're not just qualified—you're aligned.

### 3. Let the Score Speak—Use Numbers Generously

***Examples (Mid to Senior):***

- **Sales:** 'Grew eastern region revenue by 42 per cent in 18 months—₹14 crore.'
- **HR:** 'Resolved 45+ ER cases; reduced turnaround time from nine to five days.'
- **IT:** 'Reduced incident response time by 45 per cent through automation of escalation protocols.'
- **Operations:** 'Cut packaging defect rate from 3.2 per cent to 1.1 per cent using lean intervention.'

***Examples (Freshers):***

- 'Top five rank in a batch of 180.'
- 'Internship project led to 25 per cent reduction in ticket response time at XYZ Startup.'
- 'Won campus business plan contest among 350 participants.'

### 4. Craft the First-Over Impact—Write a Killer Summary

☑ ***Dos:***

- Keep it within three to five lines.
- Mention domain, experience, top skills.
- End with a strong, unique value proposition.

***Examples:***

- **Senior HR:** 'ER and IR professional with 17+ years' experience across manufacturing clusters. Led eight settlements, zero man-days lost. Strong in compliance audits and employee trust-building.'

- **IT Fresher:** 'BTech in computer science with internship in data analytics; automated reporting using Python scripts, reducing processing time by 40 per cent. Fast learner with strong fundamentals.'

**5. Highlight the Impact—Don't Just List Tasks**

***Use 'What–How–Result' Formula:***

'What you did' + 'How you did it' + 'What was the result'

***Examples (Senior):***

- **Marketing:** 'Revamped GTM plan for rural product; led to ₹3.5 crore sales in six months.'
- **HR:** 'Implemented grievance dashboard at five plants; 77 per cent closure rate under seven days.'
- **Operations:** 'Spearheaded TPM Phase 1 rollout across unit; OEE improved by 15 per cent.'

***Examples (Fresher):***

- 'Created CRM dashboard in Excel for NGO; reduced donor follow-up lag by 50 per cent.'
- 'Led 10-member fest team; managed ₹2.2 lakh budget, 1,000+ footfall.'
- 'Designed internal HR newsletter for ABC Corp during internship—appreciated by leadership.'

**6. Avoid Cracks in the Pitch—Share What Matters, Skip the Distractions**

In cricket, even a well-prepared pitch can become risky if it's not maintained. Similarly, your resume must have just the right amount of personal information—enough to help the employer assess fitness, but not so much that it distracts from your core professional value.

**Include only what adds value to hiring decisions**

***Essential (Especially for Experienced Professionals):***

- **Marital Status:** Gives context around relocation flexibility, work-life balance expectations, and occasionally, stability indicators.
- **Current CTC and Expected CTC:** Helps HR assess compensation alignment upfront—saves time for both parties.
- **Notice Period:** Crucial for project-based or urgent hiring roles.
- **Language Proficiency:** Particularly important for region-specific or global roles.
- **Certifications:** PMP, SHRM, CFA, Digital Marketing, Six Sigma, etc.
- **Technical Tools:** SAP, Power BI, Python, Canva, etc.

***Example:***

**Marital Status:** Married (Willing to Relocate)

**Current CTC:** ₹12.4 LPA | Expected: ₹15–16 LPA | Notice Period: 60 Days

***Optional or Context-specific (Use Judgement):***

- **Date of Birth or Age:** Not always needed unless the JD specifies age brackets or experience level bands
- **Nationality:** Add only if you're applying for international roles or roles requiring visa clarity

***Avoid (Unless Asked or Contextually Required):***

- Father's name
- Religion, caste, gender (unless you're applying under a specific diversity category)
- Generic hobbies (like 'watching movies' or 'surfing the internet')

**Tip for Freshers:** You can still include a crisp personal section, but keep the emphasis on relevance and maturity.

***Example:***

**Marital Status:** Single | Willing to Relocate | Languages: English, Hindi, Bengali | Certified in Google Analytics and Digital Marketing | Available for immediate joining

***Bottom Line:***

Just like a pitch report includes key factors like weather and grass coverage, your personal info section should share what matters to the game's strategy—not family history.

Let your resume pitch be insightful, structured and strategically informative.

**7. Roll It Smoothly—Make It ATS-friendly and Error-free**

Applicant Tracking Systems (ATS) screen resumes before humans do.

***Ensure:***

- **File Format:** .docx or .pdf
- **Standard Headings:** Experience | Education | Skills
- **Avoid:** Tables, text boxes, graphics
- Grammar and Spell-check (Tools: Grammarly, Hemingway)

## YOUR RESUME IS A LIVING DOCUMENT

Like a cricket pitch that evolves through sessions and seasons, your resume must be reviewed, updated and internalized. It's not a file you update once a year—it's a living reflection of who you are.

**Practise These Habits**

- Read your resume at least once every two weeks.
- Update every new project, achievement, skill, etc., immediately.
- Be aware of every word, comma and full stop.
- Ask yourself: *'Does this line reflect my current value?'*

**In an interview, you'll be asked about anything on your resume. Know it by heart. If it doesn't feel real, remove it.**

**Is the Pitch Getting Played?**

***Self-check questions:***

- Have you received one to two recruiter calls in the last three months?
- Are your bullets aligned with industry trends?
- Are your key achievements updated?

If not—revisit the pitch. Roll it again.

## FINAL WORD: LAY THE PITCH, WIN THE MATCH

You can't control who interviews you. But you **can** control the pitch you lay.

Whether you are a fresher hoping to debut, or a seasoned player ready for your next challenge, your resume should create conditions where you dominate.

*The match is long, but the tone is always set in the first over.*

## IS YOUR PITCH MATCH-READY?

Before you move on, pause and examine the pitch you've laid. In the real world, recruiters don't wait for conditions to improve—you either play on what's prepared, or you don't play at all.

1. ***10-Second Test***

   If a recruiter scans your resume for 10 seconds, what three things will stand out?

   1. ______________________________

   2. ______________________________

   3. ______________________________

   *If this isn't obvious, nothing else matters.*

2. ***Alignment Check***

   Think of the last job you applied to:

   1. Which two keywords or skills did that JD emphasize?

      ______________________________

2. Can you substantiate every claim on your résumé with clear evidence?

   ☐ Yes ☐ No

If 'No', the resume isn't ready.

3. ***Impact Check***

Scan your resume and count:

1. How many bullets show numbers, outcomes or measurable change?

   ______________________________

2. How many lines only describe activity, not impact?

   ______________________________

3. Convert two task statements into impact statements:

   ______________________________

   ______________________________

*If it mattered, it moved something. Measure it.*

4. ***48-Hour Action***

One change you will make to your resume in the next 48 hours:

______________________________

**Reminder:** *A resume is not a record of effort—it's a signal of value. Lay the pitch well. The game will follow.*

# 2

# Using SWOT to Shape Your Interview Strategy

*You don't rise to the level of your goals; you fall to the level of your preparation.*

**—James Clear**

When a batsman walks into the crease, he doesn't think about playing every ball perfectly. He thinks: *'What's my strong area? Where might I get out? What's the bowler's plan? What are my chances here?'*

A good interview strategy demands the same self-awareness. And there's no better tool than SWOT analysis to bring clarity.

## WHY SWOT?

Most candidates prepare randomly. They may think through a few common questions, memorize answers and hope for the best. But is that really enough?

After all, interviews are performance zones, not memory tests. In those few critical seconds you get to think and respond, you cannot afford to rely on luck—regardless of the level you are interviewed for.

You need a method. You need preparation.

And the best way to prepare is by knowing yourself deeply—your capabilities, vulnerabilities and how you fit the role.

That's where **SWOT** comes in. It's not just a corporate tool—it's a mirror to your professional self.

A personal SWOT gives you a 360-degree view of your profile:

- What will you showcase?
- What might you get asked about?
- How will you differentiate yourself?
- Where might you fumble?

Let's decode it.

**S—Strengths: Skills that Sell**

***Ask yourself:***

- What are you genuinely good at?
- Which achievements make you stand out?
- What do peers or mentors often appreciate about you?

**Your goal:** Build your opening pitch and response themes around these.

You may be good in the IR domain in HR or in motor maintenance within electrical engineering. Whatever your space, identify specifics. Don't just say 'I'm hardworking' or 'I'm a team player'. Bring measurable proof.

***Example (Experienced):***

'*I am good at leading teams and delivering on high-stake targets. In my last assignment, I led a sales team of 20 across the North*

*Zone and exceeded our quarterly target by 25 per cent despite supply-chain disruptions.'*

***Example (Fresher):***

Which chapters or domains do you feel most confident in? Identify that and subtly steer the interviewer in that direction: *'I've studied power electronics in detail and recently simulated a converter circuit that optimized voltage flow. I'd love to apply that learning in real-time projects.'*

***Another Example (Experienced):***

*'In my current role in supply-chain operations, I built a dashboard to track logistics delays in real time—it reduced delivery lapses by 30 per cent. Problem-solving under pressure is my biggest strength.'*

***Another Example (Fresher):***

*'During my final year engineering project, I automated a solar panel cleaning system. My team won a national innovation award. I realized I am good at translating ideas into practical prototypes.'*

**W—Weaknesses: Don't Hide, Prepare**

The question isn't whether you have weaknesses. Everyone does.

The real question is: Have you worked on them?

If not, start now.

- Identify your real gaps.
- Challenge them.
- Fortify those weak spots through learning and exposure.

The resources are all around you—your boss, colleagues, mentors, peers, YouTube, books, the internet. But the starting point is honest self-assessment.

Suppose you are well-versed in mechanical systems but lack exposure to automation. Instead of sidestepping it during interviews, start addressing it. If you are working, speak to your manager—ask to support a project involving automation, even as a secondary resource. Volunteer, stretch yourself, observe and contribute.

If that's not possible, take initiative outside work—enrol in short courses, watch expert tutorials online and reach out to domain professionals. Whatever the route, take responsibility for closing the gap.

You *cannot* walk into an interview and say, '*I don't know,*' when the job description clearly demands that knowledge. At that point, the fault is yours—for not preparing.

And most importantly—don't bluff.

If you're unsure of an answer, say: '*I'll need to cross-check,*' or '*I'd like to revisit that area before giving a firm response.*' It shows maturity and earns respect.

Think of Sourav Ganguly—brilliant through the off-side, yet initially vulnerable to short-pitched bowling. He didn't hide it. He worked on it. That's what true professionals do.

Even the best has weaknesses. But what sets them apart is that they prepare, adapt and overcome.

### O—Opportunities: Spot the Openings

Opportunities aren't just what the world gives you. They're also how you frame what you have done.

- Think of any project or assignment where you added value.

- Certifications, recognitions or even informal appreciation—everything counts.
- Your job is to package them as compelling proof of potential.

***Example (Experienced):***

Suppose you're a mechanical engineer and you handled a major plant shutdown. You planned the shutdown meticulously, reduced downtime from 30 days to 22, and saved ₹2 crores in the process. This not only ensured market delivery but also gave you a bullet point that positions you for a project head role. Lead the interview with it.

***Example (Fresher):***

'*During my internship at a manufacturing firm, I noticed excessive downtime due to manual inspections. I suggested implementing QR-code based checklists which reduced inspection time by 20 per cent. It was a small idea but one that got appreciated—and that's what I plan to highlight.*'

**T—Threats: Anticipate and Counter**

Your threats may include:

- Lack of a tier-1 college degree
- Limited exposure to industry tools or practices
- Gaps in employment or too many job switches

The key is not to panic—but to anticipate, acknowledge, and have a strategy.

Think of cricket again. If you know the opposition's spinner always gets you out, won't you prepare in advance?

Do the same here.

***Example (Experienced):***

*'Yes, I acknowledge there's some instability in my career path. Initially, I was exploring roles to find the right fit. But in the last five years, I've stayed with my current organization, grown within, and handled multiple verticals. I've matured, and now I seek depth over drift.'*

***Example (Fresher):***

*'I come from a non-metro college and don't have the exposure that tier-1 institutes offer. But I've done my bit—I interned with two reputed companies, built a solid portfolio, and maintained a blog where I discuss industry case studies and innovations. I let my work speak.'*

## CLOSING NOTE: FROM ANALYSIS TO ADVANTAGE

Most candidates walk into interviews and react. You'll walk in prepared and proactive—because you have done your SWOT.

This tool doesn't just prepare you to answer questions—it gives you the power to **steer** them. And that's what real performers do.

Like a batsman who reads the field and paces the innings, a great candidate knows it's not about perfection—it's about clarity, control and character.

*SWOT helps you master all three.*

## TURN SWOT INTO STRATEGY

Reading about SWOT is easy. Using it under pressure is what separates preparation from performance. Pause here, and do the work.

**1. *Your One-Line SWOT***

Be specific. No jargon. No exaggeration.

**Strengths (What you should lead with):**
What skills, experiences or achievements genuinely differentiate you?

___

**Weaknesses (What you must prepare for):**
What gaps could an interviewer probe—and how are you addressing them?

___

**Opportunities (What you should highlight):**
Which projects, results or recognitions position you for the *next* role?

___

**Threats (What you must anticipate):**
What aspects of your profile could work against you—and how will you counter them?

___

**2. *Pressure-Test Your Preparation***

Ask yourself:

- If this interview goes *slightly off-script*, do I still know how to respond?
- Can I link my strengths directly to the job's expectations?
- Have I prepared responses for uncomfortable but predictable questions?

Interviews don't reward perfection. They reward preparedness.

**3. *Final Commitment***

Complete this sentence:

**'Based on my SWOT, the one thing I will work on before my next interview is...'**

______________________________________________________

Then act on it.
Most candidates react in interviews.
Prepared candidates respond.
Strategic candidates *steer*.

# 3

# Smart Job Hunting: Finding the Right Opportunities

In a hyperconnected world full of job portals, recruiters, referrals and networking events, you might think it's easier than ever to land a job. But here's the catch: Access doesn't equal alignment. The smartest professionals don't just chase vacancies—they target opportunities. They don't apply everywhere—they apply strategically.

**Access doesn't guarantee alignment. Visibility doesn't ensure value.**

So, what separates random searching from smart hunting? Let's understand the approach.

### 1. Stop Applying. Start Aligning.

Most candidates begin their job search on a hopeful note but soon end up fatigued—exhausted by repetitive applications, silence from recruiters, and interviews that go nowhere.

Why? Because they play the volume game instead of the value game. A smarter approach is:

- **Know your 'Why':** Are you solving for growth, culture fit, upskilling, location or compensation?
- **Decode the JD:** Go beyond titles. Study the KRAs,

skillsets, values and tone. Read between the lines.

- **Map it to your SWOT:** Does the role use your strengths? Help fix weaknesses? Align with your long-term path?

You're not trying to win every match. You're choosing the ones where you're best positioned to score.

**Read the pitch before swinging the bat.**

A great batsman doesn't start swinging at every ball. They first assess the pitch, study the field, understand the bowler—and then play their shots. Job search is no different. Read the JD. Study the industry. Understand the employer's expectations. Then make your move.

Just as a batsman chooses which deliveries to leave, defend or attack, a job seeker must pick where to invest effort—not every opening deserves your energy.

**2. Use the Power of the Hidden Job Market**

Not every opportunity is posted. In fact, many of the most rewarding roles are filled silently—through referrals, networks, internal movement or discreet headhunting.

To tap into this hidden market:

- **LinkedIn Strategy:** Optimize your profile. Post occasionally about your domain. Engage with industry-relevant content. Build connections—especially with mid-level professionals, HR leaders and talent acquisition teams.

**Smart Tip:** Don't just collect connections—*build credibility.* People refer those who are visible and trusted.

During a job search, even when you actively reach out to your LinkedIn connections, most remain silent or offer only vague responses—often due to their own constraints. But it only takes one positive reply, which may become the stepping stone to your next opportunity.

- **Networking:** One of the major pillars of a smart job search. Stay in touch with your former bosses, HR managers, mentors and college seniors. Drop in a '*Hi, how are you doing?*' message every now and then. Chit-chat often or on occasion.
- People forget you if you go silent.
- Relationships fade if they are not nurtured.
- And no one wants to be contacted only when you need a job.

I am writing this from my own experience. During a particularly challenging phase in my career, when I was actively exploring new opportunities, it wasn't a portal or a recruiter that proved most helpful—it was one of my former bosses. I maintained a positive rapport with a senior leader in an organization, even after I had left it. When I reached out, he not only responded but extended genuine support and helped me secure the right opportunity. That moment reaffirmed a timeless truth: Real professional relationships matter. And they are best built before you need them—through mutual respect, authenticity and consistent connection.

**Pro Tip:** Never exit a company on bitter terms. Today's goodbye may become tomorrow's return ticket.

**3. Track Trends. Don't Just Chase Titles.**

Job titles are evolving. Entire functions are being reshaped. Today's job may disappear tomorrow—or transform beyond recognition.

Stay ahead by watching:

- **Emerging roles:** ESG, DEI, employer branding, HR analytics, legal ops, digital wellness.
- **Hybrid functions:** Law + Data, HR + Tech, Ops + Analytics.
- **Workplace models:** Hybrid, remote-first, async teams, gig-based structures.

The best candidates don't just respond to change—they anticipate it.

Stay alert, like a skilled fielder—because opportunity doesn't always arrive at the expected position.

**4. Build a Target List (Diversify like an Investor)**

Treat your job search like a well-managed investment portfolio—diverse, balanced and consistently reviewed.

Don't rely on one job board or recruiter. Spread your efforts across:

- **Portals:** Naukri, LinkedIn Jobs, Times Jobs, iimjobs, Hirist, Indeed, Monster. Everyone has opinions—some say this portal is best, some say another. Don't rely on one. Optimize from all.
- **Recruiters:** Especially domain-focused head-hunters.
- **Referrals:** Alumni, ex-colleagues, friends.
- **Company pages:** Track your 'Top 15' companies. Visit their 'careers' pages regularly.
- **Professional forums:** WhatsApp/Telegram industry groups.

Just as a wise investor diversifies across equities, debt and gold, a job seeker must balance portals, referrals and recruiters.

Maintain a tracker:

- Where you've applied
- Contact person (if known)
- Follow-up date
- Status and next steps

It's your job search dashboard—treat it like a scorecard.

**5. Prepare before You Are Desperate**

The worst time to prepare for a job is after you've already left one.

Build momentum before you need it:

- Update your resume quarterly.
- Refresh your Naukri or other portal profiles every seven days to stay visible.
- Track achievements and KPIs regularly.
- Attend one learning event or alumni meet every quarter.
- Stay active in your domain circles.

You don't fix your bat grip after getting out. You work on it between innings.

Likewise, you sharpen your career tools before you're at the crease again.

## FINAL THOUGHT: CHOOSE. DON'T CHASE.

Smart job hunting is not about frantic motion—it's about focused direction.

You're not just seeking a job. You're offering a solution—a unique blend of skills, experience and attitude.

When that mindset shifts:

- Your messages become confident, not needy.
- Your resume becomes a pitch, not a diary.
- Your interviews become conversations, not interrogations.

∽

**ARE YOU HUNTING—OR JUST SEARCHING?**

Job hunting feels busy. Smart job hunting feels deliberate. Pause here and examine how you are actually approaching your search.

1. ***Alignment Check: Why Am I Looking?***

   Answer honestly—no generic answers.

   - **What am I primarily solving for right now?** (Growth, compensation, learning, stability, location, culture, role clarity)

     ______________________________

   - **One thing I will not compromise on in my next role:**

     ______________________________

Clarity here saves months of misaligned effort.

2. ***Application Reality Check***

Look at your last five applications:

- How many were **clearly aligned** with your strengths and career direction? ________ / 5
- How many were sent out of urgency, pressure or fear of missing out? ________ / 5

If urgency is driving your applications, fatigue will follow.

3. ***Targeting Test: Am I Focused?***

- **My Top 3 target roles:**

  ______________________________

- **My Top 5 target companies:**

  ______________________________

- **The one capability I want my next role to strengthen:**

  ______________________________

Random effort *feels* productive. Focused effort *is* productive. Smart job hunting is not about chasing every opening. It's about choosing where your effort compounds.

# 4

# Be Ready to Impress: Preparing for the Pre-Screening Call

*Momentum is built before the scoreboard moves. The pre-screening call is that quiet first ball—often overlooked, but it can set the tone for everything that follows.*

### Why the Pre-Screening Call Matters

Whether you have applied for a job or your profile has been found by a recruiter, the **pre-screening call is your first audition**. It may not last long, but it creates a lasting impression.

### What Recruiters Look for:

- Relevance to the role
- Communication clarity
- Seriousness and preparedness
- Willingness to move forward

**Your Goal?**
Don't oversell. Don't play it cool. Just be genuinely interested, informed and clear-headed.

## Two Paths to the Call

Let's understand the two different contexts in which a pre-screening call usually happens—and how your mindset must shift accordingly.

### *Scenario 1: You Applied for the Job*

In this case, you know the company and the role. So, you must:

- Be ready with a crisp summary of why you applied.
- Revisit the job description before the call.
- Match your experience to key requirements.
- Express clear intent to move forward if it fits.

This is like walking out to bat after reading the pitch report. You have had time. Use it well.

### *Scenario 2: You Are Being Approached (Resume Uploaded or Sourced)*

Here, the recruiter may catch you off guard. You may not know the company or role in advance. That's okay.

Your approach should be:

- Stay calm and curious.
- Politely ask for details about the role.
- Listen actively and don't bluff.
- If it interests you, show willingness to engage further.

This is like being called to bat mid-match. You didn't expect it—but your readiness shows in how you adapt.

## Sample Dialogue: Pre-Screening Done Right

Let's look at a simple yet effective conversation where the

candidate handles the call with confidence and curiosity—even with limited prior information.

**Recruiter:** Hi, this is Priya calling from Zeon Technologies. You had applied for the position of business analyst a few days ago through LinkedIn. Is now a good time to speak?

**Candidate:** *Yes, absolutely. Thank you for calling. I do remember applying for the business analyst role—I would be glad to discuss.*

**Recruiter:** Great! Just to give you a quick overview—the role is based in Bangalore, and it's part of our digital transformation team. We're looking for someone with strong analytical capabilities, stakeholder communication, and ideally some exposure to automation tools. Do you have a few minutes to talk about your background?

**Candidate:** *Certainly. From what you have shared, it sounds quite aligned. In my current role at a retail analytics firm, I handle cross-functional reporting and recently worked on an automation project using Power BI and Excel macros. I would be happy to share more.*

**Recruiter:** That's good to know. Can you quickly walk me through your experience and what brings you to the job market?

**Candidate:** *Sure. I have spent the last three years in client-facing analytics roles—primarily focused on operations efficiency and reporting dashboards. Recently, I have been looking to move into a role where I can work closer with transformation teams and bring a stronger tech angle to the solutions I build. When I saw this opening at Zeon, it struck* *that balance of business understanding and digital capability.*

**Recruiter:** Sounds relevant. Is there any particular reason you are exploring a change?

**Candidate:** *Mostly career progression. My current role has been great for building a foundation, but I am looking to work in a setup that's scaling rapidly and offers scope to lead projects. Also, the idea of being part of a transformation team is very motivating to me.*

**Recruiter:** Understood. Lastly, do you have any initial questions?

**Candidate:** *Just one for now—could you share a bit about the team structure or how success is measured in this role?*

**Recruiter:** Sure. The role reports to the transformation head and interacts directly with operations and IT. Success is usually tracked through automation savings, adoption rate, and process improvement timelines.

**Candidate:** *That's really helpful, thank you. It sounds like an exciting role, and I'd be very interested in moving ahead if you feel there's a match.*

**Note:** While the above dialogue is illustrative, it closely reflects how recruiters usually structure pre-screening conversations. The tone, flow and expectations remain similar—only the domain, level and function vary. Your responses should follow the same spirit of clarity, relevance and interest—tailored to your background.

**Freshers—Sample Questions:**

For freshers, questions may include:

- Can you walk me through your academic projects or internships?
- Why are you interested in this role or industry?
- Have you taken any certifications or online courses relevant to this role?
- Are you open to relocation or flexible working hours?
- What interests you about this company or industry?
- How do you handle deadlines or multiple academic responsibilities?

The focus here is not on job experience—but on your attitude, awareness and adaptability. And just like experienced candidates, freshers should stay composed, communicate clearly, and express a genuine willingness to learn.

**First Call Strategy in 5 Steps:**

1. ***Stay Calm, Not Caught off Guard***
   Whether expected or not, respond politely and professionally.

2. ***Seek Clarity, then Respond***
   Ask for role details if not known. Listen actively.

3. ***Show Positive Interest***
   Express why the role or company excites you—once you understand it.

4. ***Align Experience Briefly***
   Link your key skills or project highlights to what's shared.

5. ***Ask a Thoughtful Question***
Even one meaningful question shows maturity and depth.

## FINAL WORD: NOT JUST A CALL—A CUE

Think of the pre-screening call as the toss in a cricket match. You don't win the game at the toss—but the tone is set. The way you observe, respond and align in that short moment affects what follows.

A well-prepared toss moment isn't just about calling heads or tails—it's about understanding the pitch, the weather and your strengths. That's exactly what you do on a pre-screening call.

Whether you applied or got approached, the pre-screening call is your first cue to set the tone.

You may not control *when* it comes, but you can control *how* you show up.

Be curious. Be composed. Be clear.

And just like the best players—*treat every ball like it could be the breakthrough*.

# 5

# Before the Big Day: What You Must Know

*Preparation isn't just part of the game. It is the game.*

An interview doesn't begin when you enter the room. It begins the moment you decide to show up as the best version of yourself. And that means knowing three things before the big day:

- The company you are meeting
- The role you're being considered for
- The person who might be asking the questions

*Let's decode each.*

## 1. Know the Company: Don't Just Visit the Website—Understand the Why

Many candidates read the company's 'About Us' and think they are done. But in the interview room, general knowledge isn't enough—insight is power.

***Go beyond the Obvious:***

- What are the company's key products or services?
- What makes it different from its competitors?

- What are the recent developments—new markets, leadership changes, innovations?
- What do they talk about on LinkedIn or in press releases?

***Why This Matters:***

When you show you have taken the time to learn about the business, you convey curiosity, seriousness and intent. It signals that you are not just job-hunting—you are value-aligning.

A good opener doesn't wait for the first ball to read the pitch. He studies the bounce, weather, bowler stats and even what side of the seam the ball might swing. Same goes for a candidate—know the turf before stepping in.

**2. Know the Role: Read the JD, then Read between the Lines**

Most job descriptions are written like batting scorecards—facts, figures and expectations. But your job is to interpret what's underneath.

***What to Ask Yourself:***

- What are the top three deliverables in this role?
- What business problems is the company trying to solve through this position?
- What kind of person might thrive here?
- Where does this role sit in the larger structure?

***Now, Connect the Dots:***

- Highlight projects or achievements that mirror what they want.
- Don't just match skills—match intent.
- Reflect a mindset that says, '*I understand your need—and*

*I've solved similar things before.'*

### 3. Know the Interviewer: If You Know Who's Bowling, You Know Where to Guard

You won't always know your interviewer. But when you do—it's an edge.

***Where to Look:***

- LinkedIn (focus on career path, posts, interests)
- Company website bios
- Mutual connections
- Event panels, articles or forums (if they have spoken publicly)

***Why It Matters:***

Interviewers don't just assess skill—they assess compatibility. Knowing their domain helps you pitch better.

- If your interviewer is the functional head—talk impact and KPIs.
- If they are from HR—talk values, fit and team collaboration.
- If it's a senior leader—talk future readiness and problem-solving.

**Pro Tip:** Subtly tailor examples to what they value. If their background is in operations, mention process improvements or efficiency wins.

A batter adjusts based on whether he is facing spin or pace. Same with interviewers. Anticipate the 'bowler'—and adjust your stance.

**Rapid Prep Questions: Test Your Readiness**

Before the interview, pause and ask yourself these:

***About the Company:***

- What are their top three products or services?
- What's one recent headline or news item involving them?
- How do they position themselves against competitors?
- What values or culture do they seem to promote?

***About the Role:***

- What are the three most critical outcomes expected from this role?
- Which line in the JD excited you most—and why?
- What's one challenge you believe this role is trying to address?
- How does your experience map to their expectations?

***About the Interviewer:***

- What can you tell about their background from LinkedIn?
- Have they worked in similar industries or roles as you?
- What themes do they focus on—strategy, execution, innovation, team culture?
- Based on their profile, what kind of questions do you expect?

If you can confidently answer most of these, you are not just prepared—you are *poised.*

**The Day Mehul Walked in like He Already Worked There**

Mehul was interviewing for a logistic lead role at a large FMCG company. While researching, he found a recent article where the company's COO mentioned supply disruptions in Northeast units due to unreliable vendor schedules.

Instead of just talking about his achievements, Mehul said during the interview: *'I read that supply consistency in remote locations has been a challenge. At my current plant, we faced a similar issue with a rural vendor. By introducing a vendor audit calendar and dispatch buffer system, we increased our on-time dispatch rate from 78 per cent to 93 per cent within two quarters. I'd be excited to bring a similar approach here.'*

That answer changed the energy in the room.

He wasn't just a candidate anymore. He was someone who had already started thinking like an insider.

**For Freshers: No Experience? No Problem—Bring Evidence of Effort**

The smartest freshers don't pretend to know everything. They prepare to ask better questions.

When you are starting out, you may not have corporate experience—but you do have the ability to prepare deeper than most.

And that's your edge.

***What Freshers Can (and Should) Do before the Interview:***

- **Study the Company's Story:** How did it grow? What space does it dominate? What's changing in its market?
- **Understand the Function You Are Applying for:** Look up basic industry practices in your domain.
- **Go beyond the Syllabus:** Interviewers often appreciate a fresher who says, *'I read about your supply chain challenges in remote areas. I haven't worked on it, but I studied how other FMCG companies tackle it and found some ideas interesting.'*

Even that level of curiosity sets you apart.

**Pro Tip for Freshers:** When you don't have a past to showcase, use your preparation to prove your potential. Interviewers don't expect you to know everything. But they do expect you to have done your homework.

**Sample Fresher Response:** '*I may not have direct experience, but I have studied your business model and the expectations of this role. I have already looked into practical solutions used by similar companies and can see where I could apply them meaningfully here.*'

***This Shows:***

- Curiosity
- Company-specific understanding
- Role alignment
- A learner's mindset

## THE LAST WORDS: KNOW, ALIGN, CONNECT

Preparation isn't about perfection. It's about precision.

When you know the company, understand the role, and anticipate your interviewer's lens, you enter the room already halfway through the chase.

You are not there to impress.

You are there to *connect*—with the culture, the purpose and the people.

# 6

# Preparation Is Power: Thinking in Advance Wins Interviews

In cricket, preparation doesn't begin on match day. It begins in the nets, days or even weeks in advance. A batsman facing a world-class bowler doesn't walk into the crease casually—they study the pitch, anticipate the bowler's tactics, and train with intent. Interviews are no different.

An interview is not just a meeting—it is your innings. And like any good innings, it begins well before you take the field. It is a moment when aspirations collide with opportunity, and preparation decides whether you bat with confidence or struggle defensively.

## THE COST OF CASUALNESS

In my experience as an interviewer, one truth keeps resurfacing: Candidates don't falter because they lack talent. They falter because they fail to prepare.

Even seasoned professionals sometimes walk in without having read their own resumes. I've seen it firsthand. One senior candidate had a stellar resume, but when asked about his achievements, his answers were vague and unconvincing.

He hadn't thought through his own story. Naturally, he didn't move to the next round.

Let me share a contrasting moment that left a lasting impression on me that underscores the power of preparation. During a visit to our company's guesthouse, I came across handwritten notes in a drawer—lists of probable interview questions and answers. Curious, I inquired about the previous occupant of the room and learned it was a senior leader who occupied the room. A few days later, I heard he had secured a leadership role at a competitor company, one with responsibilities far greater than his current position. His success was no accident; it was a testament to his seriousness and preparation.

## WHY PREPARATION IS NON-NEGOTIABLE

1. ***It Reflects Seriousness***
   - When you prepare, it tells the interviewer that you value the opportunity. It's respect in action.

2. ***It Builds Confidence***
   - Confidence doesn't come from luck. It comes from knowing your material—your resume, your industry, your achievements.

3. ***It Sets You Apart***
   - Most candidates show up. Few show up ready. Preparation is what separates the standout from the crowd.

4. ***It Shapes Your Story***
   - Every interview is a chance to tell your story. Preparation helps you frame your narrative with clarity and relevance.

**Key Areas to Focus On**

1. ***Know Your Resume Inside-Out***
   - Treat it like your match stats. If it's on your resume, you should be ready to talk about it.
   - Be prepared for questions like:
     - Why did you make certain career transitions?
     - What challenges did you tackle in past roles?
     - What real impact did your contributions make?

2. ***Understand the Role and the Organization***
   - Study the job description. Identify the key deliverables and required skills.
   - Learn about the company's values, leadership style, recent news and culture.

3. ***Anticipate Behavioural Questions***
   - Use the STAR method (Situation, Task, Action, Result) to prepare answers.
   - Focus on examples that demonstrate problem-solving, teamwork, leadership and adaptability.

4. ***Prepare for Domain-Specific Questions***
   - Know your turf. Whether you're in finance, operations or HR, stay current with trends, tools and techniques.
   - Demonstrate not just what you have done, but how you think.

5. ***Address Weaknesses Strategically***
   - Be honest but constructive. If you have gaps, prepare a mature narrative around them (e.g., upskilling, personal responsibilities).
   - Don't bluff if you don't know something. Instead say,

*'That's an area I am actively exploring,'* or, *'I am happy to deep dive and apply myself quickly.'*

**How to Prepare Effectively**

1. ***Create a Question Bank***
   - Write down expected behavioural and functional questions. Practise your answers aloud.
2. ***Take Mock Interviews***
   - Especially useful for freshers. Seek feedback from mentors or peers.
3. ***Stay Current***
   - Follow industry news. Know what your competitors are doing.
4. ***Plan Your First Impression***
   - Dress right. Be punctual. Practise your introduction.
5. ***Rehearse, but Don't Memorize***
   - Know your points, but keep it conversational. Authenticity matters.

**Tailored Tips Based on Experience Level**

***For Freshers:***

- Know your academic projects, internships and learnings inside-out.
- Anticipate basic domain-related questions in your area of course or study.
- Research the company and express your enthusiasm clearly.
- Practise communicating clearly and confidently.

**Example:** A recent graduate once impressed a panel by linking his final-year project on data analysis with a real-time issue faced by the company, proposing a basic but effective solution. He had done his research, and it showed.

***For Mid-Level Professionals:***

- Focus on results and measurable impact in previous roles.
- Be ready to explain career transitions and growth aspirations.
- Prepare leadership and team collaboration examples.
- Study the company's performance, culture and where you fit in.

**Example:** One candidate transitioning from a regional role to a national profile walked in with a deep understanding of the company's expansion plans and mapped out how his distribution experience in tier-2 cities would support those goals. He was not just prepared—he was aligned.

***For Senior Leadership:***

- Prepare a narrative around strategic initiatives led, culture built and transformations driven.
- Expect board-level questions and macro-level problem solving.
- Be ready to speak on vision, stakeholder management, crisis handling and succession planning.
- Align your leadership philosophy with the company's future direction.

**Example:** A CXO-level candidate once began his interview by discussing a recent shift in the company's market strategy. He linked it with a similar turnaround he had led in a previous organization, citing numbers, timelines and cultural shifts. His preparation showed both business depth and leadership insight.

**Common Pitfalls to Avoid**

1. ***Overconfidence without Substance***
   - Experience doesn't excuse a lack of readiness.
2. ***Underestimating Simple Questions***
   - Prepare powerfully for 'Tell me about yourself' and 'Why this job?'
3. ***Weak Body Language***
   - Eye contact, posture and tone matter. Rehearse them.
4. ***Not Asking Questions***
   - Interviews are two-way. Have thoughtful questions for your interviewer.

**The Final Mental Drill**

Take a day or two before the interview. Reflect, rehearse and clarify your narrative.

Ask yourself:

- What makes me a strong fit for this role?
- What is my career vision and how does this job align?
- What unique value do I bring to the table?

Be ready with a crisp, confident answer for: 'Tell me about yourself.'

## CONCLUSION: PREPARATION IS RESPECT IN ACTION

Think about your favourite cricket captain. They don't just lead with talent—they lead with preparation. Similarly, great candidates don't wing interviews. They walk in knowing their game, the pitch and the opposition.

Treat every interview like a semi-final. No one ever regrets being too prepared. But many regret showing up casually.

In the end, success belongs to those who prepare like professionals and perform like champions.

Preparation is not a formality. It is your *power*.

# Part B

# ACING THE INTERVIEW

# 7

# The Introduction That Wins Interviews

Cricket has taught us many things. One of the most underrated lessons lies in its opening moments. Think of a limited-overs match—when the openers walk in, the entire stadium holds its breath. The first few overs set the tone for what follows. A confident, calculated start can lift the whole innings. A shaky one? It puts the middle order under pressure.

**Interviews are no different.**

When a candidate walks into an interview, the first question is almost always the same and will determine whether he will dominate the interview. Surprisingly, the first question is always or most of the time is same and yet the candidate falters.

## THE QUESTION: 'PLEASE INTRODUCE YOURSELF'

And just like that first over, this question holds power—not because of what is being asked, but because of how it is answered.

Most candidates treat this as a warm-up. But the smart ones—the ones who dominate the interview—treat it as their powerplay.

They come in having:

- Studied the company's pitch—its values, culture, business priorities.
- Understood the interviewer's bowling style—what the role demands, what skills are being evaluated.
- Crafted their opening shots—clear, relevant points that showcase strengths and direct the conversation toward their areas of confidence.

When they answer '*Tell me about yourself*', they are not just sharing a biography.

They are controlling the direction of the interview.

They speak with structure, clarity and relevance. They drop in achievements and insights that make the interviewer lean forward. They trigger curiosity. They invite the follow-up questions they are best equipped to answer.

And in doing so, they do what the great openers do in cricket—they take away the match in the opening phase.

So, whether you are facing the new ball on the field or the first question in an interview room, the principle remains the same:

Own the first over, and you are halfway to victory.

'*Tell me about yourself*' sounds deceptively simple, almost conversational. But don't be fooled. It's the most defining moment of your interview. Here's why:

- It sets the tone.
- It reveals your communication style.
- It gives you a chance to highlight your strengths early.
- It determines where the interviewer might focus next.

### Common Mistakes Candidates Make

Over the years, I have seen some recurring mistakes in how candidates respond:

- **Stating the obvious:** Starting with your name or where you are from. The interviewer already knows that from your resume.
- **Irrelevant personal details:** Talking about your family or how many siblings you have unless it's contextually relevant.
- **Rambling:** Jumping from one idea to another with no structure or clarity.
- **Information overload:** Trying to fit your whole resume into 90 seconds.
- **Clichés:** Saying you are 'hardworking' or 'passionate' without evidence.

These responses don't help. They dilute your impact and confuse the interviewer about what really matters.

## WHAT MAKES A GREAT INTRODUCTION?

A strong introduction is focused, relevant and intentional. It connects your journey with the role you are applying for. It builds curiosity.

But it also depends on your career stage. Let's look at two perspectives:

### For Experienced Professionals—Tell a Story of Growth

If you are an experienced professional, your introduction should establish credibility, highlight career progression, and align your strengths with the role you're applying for. Here's a simplified structure to follow:

1. ***Start with Your Current Role***
    - Clearly state your current designation, organization and responsibilities.
    - Example: '*I am currently a senior manager at XYZ Ltd, leading a 25-member team responsible for end-to-end supply chain operations.*'
2. ***Summarize Your Career Journey***
    - Trace your path from earlier roles to your present position.
    - Emphasize growth, exposure and skills developed.
    - Example: '*I began my career as a junior analyst at ABC Corp., focusing on market research, and gradually transitioned into operations management roles with increasing responsibility.*'
3. ***Highlight Key Achievements***
    - Use numbers and outcomes to make your impact tangible.
    - Example: '*I led a logistics optimization initiative that reduced costs by 20 per cent and improved delivery timelines.*'
4. ***Emphasize Strengths Relevant to the Role***
    - Tailor this part to match the expectations of the position.

      Examples:
        - Leadership and team management
        - Strategic thinking and execution
        - Negotiation and stakeholder engagement

5. ***Conclude with Brief Personal Details***
    - Mention academic qualifications and a line on personal background, if relevant.
    - Keep it crisp.
    - Example: '*I hold an MBA in operations management from XYZ University. I'm married and have one child pursuing high school.*'

**Sample Introduction (Consolidated Example):**

*'I am currently the senior manager of operations at XYZ Pvt. Ltd, where I manage a 25-member team overseeing supply chain and distribution. I began my career as an executive of operations at ABC Corp., and over the years, I have transitioned into leadership roles, primarily in operations and vendor management. One of my key achievements was leading a cost-reduction project that saved the company 20 per cent annually on logistics. I am particularly strong in negotiation and cross-functional collaboration. I hold an MBA in operations and live with my family in Mumbai.'*

This approach allows you to project maturity, clarity and relevance without sounding boastful. It sets the tone and gives the interviewer natural cues for follow-up questions.

**For Freshers: Structuring an Impactful Introduction**

As a fresher, your introduction should highlight your education, intentions and early experiences that showcase your potential. A thoughtful introduction reflects.

Here's a simple structure to follow:

1. ***Start with Your Most Recent Qualification***
    - Mention your course, university and any key academic achievement.

- Example: '*I recently completed my MBA in marketing from XYZ University, where I graduated with distinction and led the annual marketing fest.*'

2. ***Explain Why You Chose the Field***
   - Be specific—avoid vague or generic reasons.
   - Example: '*I chose marketing because I enjoy studying consumer behaviour and crafting strategies that connect brands with audiences in meaningful ways.*'

3. ***Highlight Internships or Projects***
   - Share practical exposure and its relevance to the role.
   - Example: '*During my internship at ABC Ltd, I contributed to a social-media campaign that increased engagement by 25 per cent.*'

4. ***Mention Extracurriculars That Reflect Key Skills***
   - Include leadership roles or achievements outside academics.
   - Example: '*As president of my college debate society, I enhanced my communication, quick thinking and team-coordination skills.*'

5. ***Conclude with Personal Interests or Background***
   - Keep it brief but meaningful.
   - Example: '*I come from a family of educators, which instilled a strong sense of discipline and love for continuous learning. In my free time, I enjoy blogging about digital marketing trends.*'

**Sample Introduction (Consolidated Example):**

*'I recently completed my MBA in marketing from XYZ University, where I actively organized the annual marketing fest and led*

*a team of 15. I chose marketing because I am fascinated by how brands influence consumer behaviour through storytelling. During my internship at ABC Ltd, I worked on a campaign that improved social media engagement by 25 per cent. I am also a certified Google Ads professional, which has enhanced my digital marketing skills. Outside academics, I have led the debating society, and I enjoy writing blogs on marketing trends and innovations.'*

**Avoid Generic Statements**

- Saying '*I love working with people, so I chose HR*' is too broad and often perceived as superficial.

Instead, make it specific and role-aligned:

'*I realized that HR is not just about interacting with people but about building trust and culture. During my internship, I helped design an onboarding programme that improved employee engagement, which deepened my interest in employee experience and workplace culture.*'

By framing your introduction in this way, you show not just who you are—but how you think, what you have learned, and how you intend to contribute.

**Preparing for Unexpected Scenarios**

While your goal with the first question is to spark curiosity around your strengths and steer the conversation accordingly, interviewers may still choose to explore areas outside your core expertise.

I recall an interview where I was told, 'We know Employee Relations is your forte, but tell us what you have done in the broader HR domain.'

Such moments test your readiness. You may have a specialization, but interviews often assess your functional awareness beyond your comfort zone. Saying, '*That's not my core area*,' can come across as evasive or unprepared.

Even freshers aren't immune—questions may arise from parts of the curriculum they are less confident in.

That's why it's critical to have at least a working understanding of all key aspects of your field, so you're never caught off guard by a question outside your stronghold.

Eliminate grey areas—interviews rarely follow a script.

### Final Tips to Craft a Killer Introduction

Whether you're a fresher or a veteran, remember:

- **Be strategic, not robotic:** Rehearse, but don't recite.
- **Guide the interview:** Introduce topics you want to talk about.
- **Stay within two to three minutes:** Share enough to showcase your strengths, but leave room for curiosity and follow-up questions.
- **Show enthusiasm:** Let your energy reflect your interest in the role and the company.
- **Be authentic:** Your story should reflect who you are—not what you think the interviewer wants to hear.

## CLOSING THOUGHTS: YOUR INTRODUCTION IS YOUR FIRST SHOT

The opening ball in cricket can be defended, left alone, or smashed for a boundary. The choice lies in how ready you are.

The '*Tell me about yourself* question offers a similar

opportunity. Done right, it helps you:

- Steer the conversation into your strength zone.
- Build rapport with the interviewer.
- Distinguish yourself from the rest.

So don't just prepare to answer the question—prepare to own the moment. Because the match is long, but the tone is always set in the first over.

**REHEARSAL CUE**

Before your interview, practise answering '*Tell me about yourself* out loud—once.

If it exceeds three minutes, sounds generic, or doesn't guide the conversation, refine it.

# 8

# Playing the Next Innings: Why This Job, Why Now?

One of the most pivotal questions in any interview is:

- 'Why have you applied for this job?'
- 'Why are you looking to switch from your current role?'

These aren't routine queries—they are filters. They help interviewers separate those who are moving with clarity from those drifting without direction. Whether you are a fresher or a mid-career professional, this question exposes your intent, planning and alignment.

## CHANGING TEAMS OR BATTING ORDER

In cricket, moving to a different team or batting position is never random—it's a calculated move. A player shifts up the order not for variety but for responsibility, exposure to tougher situations, or to play a pivotal role for the team.

Likewise, changing jobs must be a strategic decision, not an impulsive escape.

- Interviewers aren't just asking where you want to go—they're evaluating why now and why here.

- Are you stepping up to face the new ball—or simply walking away from a low score?

## WHY THIS QUESTION MATTERS

This question reveals more than what's on your resume:

- **Career Clarity:** Do you treat your career like a planned innings?
- **Alignment:** Do your goals match the company's vision?
- **Maturity:** Can you navigate transitions without blaming your past?
- **Motivation:** Are you driven by growth, or just salary and dissatisfaction?

**What Not to Say and What to Say Instead**

| ☒ Don't Say | ☑ Say This Instead |
|---|---|
| 'My company has a toxic culture.' | *'I have learned a lot, but now I am seeking an environment that aligns better with my values.'* |
| 'I want a better salary.' | *'I am looking for broader responsibilities that match my growth goals, with rewards that reflect impact.'* |
| 'I just want to try something new.' | *'This role represents the kind of challenge I have been preparing for.'* |

| | |
|---|---|
| 'I'm looking for change and relocation. Plus, your brand is big.' | *'I am looking for a role where I can contribute to a company's growth story and expand my own capabilities in the process.'* |

**Key Principles to Frame an Effective Answer**

**1. *Think like a Team Player***

You are not just chasing individual runs—you are joining a team. Show that you are here to create value for the organization, not just yourself.

*'I see myself contributing to your ongoing process improvements and innovation goals, while deepening my own skills in cross-functional collaboration.'*

**2. *Project Career Strategy***

Your next move must align with your three-to-five-year plan—not be a reaction to discomfort.

*'After gaining experience in core operations, I now seek exposure to cross-regional strategy and decision-making responsibilities. This role is a natural next step.'*

**3. *Stay Positive about the Past***

Respect your current employer even if you are ready to move on.

*'My current company has helped me grow in core areas. This opportunity allows me to apply that learning on a larger canvas.'*

### 4. *Highlight the Match, Not Just the Pitch*

You must show that it's not just about the opportunity—but the right opportunity.

*'The company's emphasis on continuous learning and agile problem-solving strongly aligns with my values and working style.'*

### What Makes a Great Answer Memorable?

- It reflects purpose over panic.
- It's specific, not generic.
- It resonates with the company's current strategy.
- It shows that you are not just switching employers—you are upgrading your mission.

Think of it like Virat Kohli adjusting his stance before every delivery—not because he is unsure, but because he respects every bowler, every pitch. Similarly, you must respect every opportunity enough to prepare deeply for why you are stepping into this arena.

Your next job isn't just about earning more—it's about becoming more.

### Moving from Routine to Relevance: A Plant Engineer's Pivot

I once interviewed an assistant manager-maintenance from a cement manufacturing plant. His resume showed robust technical depth—rotary kiln maintenance, VRM shutdowns, and energy audits. But his answer to '*Why this job, why now?*' left a lasting impression.

*'Over the past six years, I've managed critical maintenance functions. Lately, I have led initiatives in condition monitoring and process reliability. What draws me to your plant is its clear vision for modernization—moving beyond routine maintenance toward a culture of reliability, performance excellence and digital integration. I want to be part of that leadership shift, where engineering isn't just about fixing breakdowns but about driving sustainable efficiency and long-term value.'*

His response wasn't just well-rehearsed. It reflected purpose, preparation, and alignment.

Contrast that with another candidate who said:

*'I am looking for change and relocation. Plus, your brand is big.'*

The difference was stark:

- One had clarity and strategy.
- The other was hoping the brand name alone would carry him through.

This framing subtly shifts the focus from tools to vision—signalling that the candidate is not just a doer but **a future leader**.

**Tailored Responses**

***For Experienced Professionals***

**Focus Areas:**

- Cumulative achievements
- Shift to higher responsibility
- Strategic alignment

**Sample:**

*'In my current role, I have led process optimization projects that reduced downtime by 18 per cent. I now seek a role that challenges me across regions and functions. Your organization's ongoing transformation aligns with my interest in building scalable systems.'*

***For Freshers***

**Focus Areas:**

- Projects, internships and potential
- Curiosity and alignment

**Sample:**

*'During my academic journey, I worked on a capstone project involving predictive maintenance for manufacturing units. Your company's culture of structured mentorship and focus on engineering innovation matches my learning appetite and long-term goals.'*

**What Interviewers Are Evaluating**

| Criteria | What It Reflects |
|---|---|
| **Motivation** | Are you moving with purpose or escaping discomfort? |
| **Research** | Have you understood the company and the role? |
| **Commitment** | Are you looking for a meaningful stint or just any opportunity? |
| **Perspective** | Can you turn your past into a thoughtful narrative? |

**Dos and Don'ts**

☑ *Dos*

- Prepare like you are playing a final—know the pitch.
- Be specific. Show research.
- Talk about the match between the company's journey and yours.
- Acknowledge past learning. Respect your previous innings.

☒ *Don'ts*

- Don't badmouth your employer—it's like blaming the pitch for poor footwork.
- Don't lead with compensation—it's the scoreboard, not the strategy.
- Don't give template answers—customize like you would for each bowler.

## CLOSING THOUGHT: IT'S NOT A RESCUE ACT; IT'S YOUR NEXT INNINGS

Changing jobs isn't about abandoning the past. It's about stepping into a larger, more challenging arena where your contributions and leadership can grow.

Whether you have played Test innings or T20 knocks, the real question is—are you ready for this format, this team and this moment?

Your answer must say: '*Yes, I have done my homework. I know what I bring. And I am ready to play with purpose.*'

## WHY THIS JOB, WHY NOW?

**1. *One-Sentence Clarity***

Complete this in one sentence—no qualifiers.

I am moving from my current role because ____________

____________________, and I am moving toward this role

because ______________________________________.

*If this sounds defensive or vague, refine it.*

**2. *The Alignment Test***

Answer briefly:

- What problem does this role solve for the company right now?

  ______________________________________

- What capability of mine directly helps solve that problem?

  ______________________________________

If you can't connect these two, the move isn't ready.

**Final Reminder**

*This question is not about escape. It's about intent.*
*The best answers don't explain change. They justify timing.*

# 9

# Balancing Ambition and Stability: Acing the Career Aspiration Question

*'Where do you see yourself in five years?'*

This isn't just a career enquiry—it's a lens into how you think about growth, responsibility and alignment. It helps employers assess whether your vision complements their roadmap.

Much like a Test match, your answer must balance intent with patience, and aspiration with realism. It's not about hitting boundaries on every ball—it's about understanding the conditions, reading the bowler, and steadily building your innings.

## FOR EXPERIENCED PROFESSIONALS: ASPIRE TO EVOLVE STRATEGICALLY

You have already played a few innings in your career. Now, interviewers want to know how you plan to scale. They are not just looking for confidence—they are looking for clarity, alignment and foresight.

***What to Focus on:***

- **Strategic Growth:** Talk about taking on more complex roles or leading initiatives.
- **Organizational Alignment:** Emphasize how your goals align with the company's objectives and long-term vision.
- **Reward and Recognition:** It's fair to mention aspirations for the next promotion or a proportionate hike in CTC—as long as it's grounded in performance.
- **Team and Culture Building:** Reflect on your intent to mentor, collaborate and build strong teams.

**Sample Response:**

*'In five years, I see myself managing a small team within [domain]—taking ownership of key projects and contributing to business outcomes. I have gone through your recent work in [specific area], and I would like to be part of scaling those initiatives. With steady performance, I do hope to grow into a role that brings higher responsibility, including a promotion and a fair increase in compensation. I also enjoy coaching juniors, and I would like to contribute to a culture where people support and challenge each other to grow.'*

**A Five-Year Vision or a First-Ball Slog?**

In an interview I conducted for a mid-level operations role, a strong candidate confidently answered, '*I want to be the CEO in five years.*'

The intention was admirable—but the delivery felt premature, like a debutant batsman going for a six on the first ball.

I paused and asked, '*That's a bold vision—how do you plan to get there?*'

The candidate admitted they hadn't thought about the path—just the title.

A better response would've been:

*'In five years, I would like to lead a team, deliver on strategic priorities, and become someone the organization can rely on for performance and mentorship. If I grow consistently, a promotion and financial recognition would be part of that journey.'*

**Ambition works best when it's accompanied by awareness and alignment.**

In contrast, I once met a senior candidate in the logistics function who had this to say:

*'I have led zonal logistics teams. My next five years? I want to integrate digitized tracking, bring down turnaround time, and build a pipeline of two leaders under me. If that happens, I know the rest—growth, recognition, compensation—will follow.'*

This response stood out. Not because it was flashy, but because it showed thinking at the right altitude—from individual to systems-level.

## FOR FRESHERS: LEARN, CONTRIBUTE AND ALIGN

As a fresher, you are stepping onto the professional pitch for the first time. No one expects you to declare innings—but they do expect you to read the field, understand the game, and commit to playing it with integrity and drive.

***What to Focus on:***

- **Skill Development:** Show your eagerness to learn the ropes.

- **Team Contribution:** Highlight your readiness to add value from day one.
- **Cultural Fit and Stability:** Signal that you are here to grow—not job-hop.

**Sample Response:**

*'As a newcomer, my goal over the next five years is to build a strong foundation in [specific domain] and contribute meaningfully to my team. I am excited about the opportunity to work on live projects, learn from experienced colleagues, and steadily grow into a reliable contributor. Over time, I would like to take on more responsibility and become someone the team can count on. I see this company as a place where I can evolve and stay committed long term.'*

If you are a fresher without a fixed path in mind, say so—but back it up with curiosity and context. For example:

*'To be honest, I don't have a rigid five-year map yet. But I have researched how people grow within your company—from trainee roles into specialist tracks. I want to start by learning from the best, contribute where I can, and then carve my path from there. What matters to me is meaningful work and growing alongside a team that shares knowledge freely.'*

That kind of honesty, backed by effort, always resonates more than empty ambition.

**Common Pitfalls to Avoid**

- **Overreaching Too Soon:** Wanting to be CEO within three to five years may sound disconnected from the current role.
- **Vague or Generic Goals:** 'Let's see where life takes me' shows lack of direction.

- **Signals of Instability:** Talking about plans to switch industries, go abroad, or start your own venture too early could raise concerns.

**How to Craft the Right Answer**

- Research Internal Growth Pathways: Understand how people grow in the company.
- Match Your Ambition to Value Creation: Frame growth as something you earn by delivering outcomes.
- Contextualize It to the Role: A finance analyst and a sales lead won't have the same five-year arc.
- Be Authentic: Your tone should reflect thought—not performance.

## FINAL THOUGHTS

This question isn't about having a fixed destination—it's about knowing your direction.

Whether you are stepping into your first job or preparing for your next strategic leap, your answer should say:

'*I am not here for the ride—I am here to grow, to contribute and to stay.*'

In cricket and careers, it's not about fireworks in the first over—it's about knowing when to defend, when to drive, and when to take that game-changing single.

The most compelling candidates are not just chasing roles—they are owning their development. They treat each opportunity as part of a broader career strategy, not a stopgap.

So, before your next interview, reflect:

*What do I want to learn? Where do I want to lead? And how does this role serve that mission?*

When you answer with intent, maturity and alignment—your ambition no longer sounds like a wish. It sounds like a plan.

AMBITION WITH AWARENESS

**1. *The Five-Year Anchor***

Complete this in two lines: In five years, I want to be known in this organization as someone who ____________________ ______________________________and ____________________.

This keeps ambition role-linked, not title-driven.

**2. *The Stability Signal***

Answer honestly:

If this role goes well, what would make me stay and grow here?

______________________________________________

If the answer is unclear, the ambition may sound premature.

# 10

# Strengths, Weaknesses and Failures: Turning Answers into Advantages

In interviews, every answer you give shapes the story you tell. Learn how to turn even your vulnerabilities into a showcase of potential, resilience and growth.

Some interview questions look simple but carry enormous weight. Three of the questions mostly asked shape how candidates are judged:

- What are your strengths?
- What are your weaknesses?
- Can you describe a failure?

Handled well, they make an impact. Handled poorly, they can overshadow even the strongest resumes.

## WHY INTERVIEWERS ASK THESE QUESTIONS

| Question | What They Are Really Checking |
|---|---|
| Strengths | *How self-aware and job-aligned you are* |
| Weaknesses | *Whether you are honest, reflective and coachable* |
| Failures | *Your resilience, learning agility and accountability* |

Think of these questions as the x-ray machines at an airport. On the surface, they seem simple—just passing your bags through. But what they reveal is deeper—your strengths, vulnerabilities, and how you handle pressure. Interviewers use these questions to 'scan' not just your skills, but your core maturity.

In simple terms:

- Do you know yourself?
- Can you improve yourself?
- Can you overcome setbacks?

**How to Tackle 'What Are Your Strengths'**

***For Freshers:***

You may not have years of experience yet, but you have skills that show readiness.

- Focus on Transferable Skills: Adaptability, teamwork, problem-solving.
- Support with an Example: Let your strengths emerge through real actions.

**Example:**

'*Adaptability is one of my key strengths. In my final-year project, when unexpected data errors disrupted our timeline, I quickly learned new analytical tools and helped salvage the project. We not only met the deadline but earned top grades. It taught me to stay calm under pressure and adapt quickly.*'

***For Experienced Professionals:***

- **Highlight Business Impact:** Strengths should be tied to outcomes.

- **Align Closely to the Role:** Choose strengths that matter to the interviewer.

**Example:**

'*One of my strengths is leading cross-functional teams under pressure. At my last role as unit head, I spearheaded a cost-saving project that cut operational expenses by 15 per cent within six months, by aligning departments around a unified goal.*'

**Think of strengths like the foundation of a building.**

If the foundation is strong but hidden, it holds up the structure. But in an interview, you must bring your foundation into view—through real examples—so the interviewer can trust what they are hiring will last.

**How to Tackle 'What Are Your Weaknesses?'**

- This question is not about exposing flaws.
- It's about showing self-awareness and growth.

***For Freshers:***

- **Choose a Non-damaging Weakness:** Pick something developmental.
- **Focus on Your Improvement Efforts:** Action matters more than confession.

**Example:**

'*Initially, I found it difficult to ask for help, thinking I had to solve everything myself. But working on group projects taught me that collaboration leads to stronger outcomes. Now, I proactively seek input when needed, without hesitation.*'

***For Experienced Professionals:***

- Select a Professional Weakness: Nothing personal or trivial.
- Show the Correction Path: How you recognized and addressed it.

**Example:**

'*Earlier in my leadership career, I sometimes hesitated to initiate difficult conversations about underperformance, thinking that individuals would self-correct over time. However, I realized that delaying feedback only made situations harder. Over time, I consciously worked on addressing concerns early—setting clear expectations, offering support, and ensuring that issues were handled with respect and urgency.*'

**Personal Anecdote: Handling the Weakness Question**

In the early years of my career, when asked about my weakness, I would often default to saying, '*I am a workaholic*.' At the time, it felt safe—something that sounded like a strength disguised as a flaw. But over the years, I realized that seasoned interviewers look for authenticity, not rehearsed answers.

Through reflection, I understood that my real area of growth was learning to manage energy, not just time. I tended to stretch myself thin across multiple projects, believing that effort alone guaranteed outcomes.

Today, when asked about weaknesses, I share a more genuine insight. I explain how I learned the importance of prioritization, saying 'NO' politely but firmly, while also collaborating. For example, in one such interview I said, 'I was asked by a department head to approve a hurried, non-compliant hiring request. Earlier, I might have taken it on to avoid confrontation. But this time, I respectfully explained the need to follow due process and proposed an alternative timeline. I said, "I understand the urgency, but it's important we align with policy to protect both the candidate's interest and the organization's standards. Let's work together to find a compliant solution quickly." The conversation stayed positive—and we closed the requirement properly without compromising compliance.'

This shift from giving a 'perfect' answer to giving a real answer has helped me build deeper credibility when faced with such questions.

**How to Tackle 'Can You Describe a Failure'**

Failures reveal resilience. Growth emerges from how you handle setbacks.

***For Freshers:***

- **Choose a Low-Stakes Example:** Academic or early work experiences.
- **Emphasize Learning:** What changed because of the experience.

**Example:**

'*During an inter-college competition, I led a team without clarifying everyone's roles. As a result, execution was chaotic, and we missed winning. It taught me that clear role definition upfront is critical—a principle I now always apply in team settings.*'

***For Experienced Professionals:***

- **Pick a Professional Situation:** Keep it relevant and work-focused.
- **Own the Mistake, Highlight the Fix:** Accountability earns respect.

**Example:**

'*During a customer-experience-transformation project, I concentrated extensively on external improvements but underestimated the importance of aligning our internal IT team early. This caused avoidable technical delays. Recognizing the issue, I initiated structured cross-functional meetings, ensured consistent updates, and realigned efforts. The project recovered successfully, and it reinforced my belief that internal collaboration is as critical as external outcomes.*'

**Think of failure as falling while learning to ride a bicycle.**

You don't succeed by never falling—you succeed by adjusting your balance after every fall. The goal is not to avoid failure altogether but to minimize damage, recover fast, and become more stable with every attempt.

**Pro Interview Tips**

When sharing a weakness or failure, don't just narrate the incident—highlight the correction. Interviewers are less interested in what went wrong and more impressed by what you did next.

***Pitfalls to Avoid***

- **Over-Bragging on Strengths:** Be specific and grounded, not boastful.

- **Cliches in Weaknesses:** Avoid '*I work too hard*' or similar rehearsed lines.
- **Blaming Others in Failures:** Always take ownership—it signals leadership maturity.

*Use the STAR Method*

Keep your answers sharp and structured:

- Situation—Set the context.
- Task—Define your responsibility.
- Action—Explain what you did.
- Result—Share the outcome and learning.

## FINAL REFLECTION

Weakness shared with maturity shows strength—and the readiness to lead better tomorrow than yesterday.

- Handling the strength, weakness and failure questions is about showing that you are self-aware, growth-minded and resilient.
- Prepare with honesty. Reflect deeply. Answer with clarity.

And you will stand out not for being flawless—but for being truly future-ready.

## TURN VULNERABILITY INTO ADVANTAGE

**1.** ***Pick Your STAR Stories***

Write down **one story** for each. Be specific.

**Strength (what I reliably deliver):**

___

**Weakness (what I actively manage better now):**

___

**Failure (what reshaped my approach):**

___

**2.** ***Credibility Check***

Tick only if true for **each story**:

- ☐ I take ownership (no blame-shifting).
- ☐ The learning is clear and real.
- ☐ I can explain how this changed how I work today.

If any box remains unchecked, refine the story.

**3.** ***Growth Line***

Complete this sentence: This experience made me a better professional because ___

___

# 11

# The Art of Answering Competency-based Questions

Competency-based interview questions are designed to assess how candidates apply specific skills, behaviours and attitudes in real-world scenarios. Rather than focusing purely on technical knowledge, these questions delve into how individuals handle challenges, collaborate with others, solve problems, and demonstrate leadership. They are based on a simple but powerful principle: Past behaviour is one of the strongest predictors of future performance.

Typically introduced with prompts like '*Tell me about a time when...*' or '*Describe a situation where you...*' competency-based questions have become a cornerstone of structured interviews, especially for leadership and experienced roles. However, fresh graduates must also be prepared to navigate them—drawing from academic, internship or volunteer experiences.

Mastering these questions equips candidates at all career stages to showcase their abilities with confidence and clarity.

## WHY COMPETENCY QUESTIONS MATTER IN INTERVIEWS

Competency-based questions serve two critical purposes for employers:

- **Predicting Future Success:** They help assess whether a candidate possesses the competencies necessary to thrive in the role.
- **Aligning with Organizational Values:** They enable evaluation of traits such as teamwork, initiative, strategic thinking and cultural fit.

For leadership roles, competency assessments often focus on strategic vision, decision-making, team empowerment, and partnership-building. For freshers, the lens may shift slightly to potential, adaptability and learnability—but the fundamental expectation remains: How effectively can the candidate translate competencies into action?

### Core Competencies Interviewers Look for

Certain competencies are universally valued, especially for leadership and high-impact positions. Here's an overview:

- **Entrepreneurial Mindset:** Ability to drive innovation, take calculated risks, and deliver results amidst ambiguity.
- **Fostering a Growth Mindset:** Demonstrating openness to learning, resilience to change, and inspiring continuous improvement in teams.
- **Building Partnerships:** Collaborating across functions, building trust, and aligning diverse stakeholders towards shared objectives.

- **Demonstrating Resourcefulness:** Solving problems creatively, navigating constraints, and optimizing available resources.
- **Empowering Teams:** Delegating authority wisely, building ownership, and nurturing the growth of others.
- **Developing Impactful Insights:** Translating data into strategic decisions through critical analysis and practical foresight.
- **Being Strategic:** Planning long-term, prioritizing effectively, and aligning actions with broader organizational goals.
- **Exhibiting Confidence:** Displaying self-assurance, decisiveness and resilience under pressure.

## Structuring Your Answers: The STAR Framework

We have already learned about the **STAR (Situation, Task, Action, Result)** framework in Chapter 10. Let us see how it works in action through an anecdote:

### Leadership under Pressure

Some years ago, I was part of the final interview panel for a unit head position at one of our major manufacturing sites. This site had a history of operational disruptions, union unrest, and slipping compliance scores. We needed someone who could not only stabilize operations but rebuild trust with employees and external stakeholders.

During the interviews, one candidate with extensive plant leadership experience came in. On paper, he seemed ideal. However, when asked to describe a time he managed a critical operational crisis, his response lacked depth. He spoke about '*being available for the team*' and '*pushing for improvements*', but gave no specifics—no real sense of the situation, the actions he personally took, or the measurable results achieved.

We listened, but the narrative felt generic. We couldn't visualize his leadership during adversity.

Later, another candidate arrived—less flamboyant on paper but vastly more grounded. When we asked about handling an operational crisis, he structured his answer almost unconsciously using the STAR framework:

- **Situation:** He detailed a machinery failure incident at a previous plant, which risked halting production during a peak demand period.
- **Task:** He had been tasked with ensuring minimal downtime while simultaneously negotiating with customers and internal teams to manage expectations.
- **Action:** He explained how he set up a crisis management team within 24 hours, prioritized alternate production lines, arranged emergency vendor support, and personally held daily review meetings with cross-functional teams and customers.
- **Result:** Not only did the plant resume 80 per cent of operations within 48 hours, the unit even achieved a monthly dispatch record the following month, restoring confidence internally and externally.

The clarity, the structure, and the authenticity of his storytelling made the entire panel sit up.

He didn't just narrate a role—he made us experience his leadership under pressure.

In leadership hiring, this makes the difference: Competency without clarity leads to doubt. Competency with structured clarity breeds trust.

Notably, through this one example, the candidate demonstrated several critical leadership competencies:

- **Handling Operational Crisis and Resourcefulness:** His swift and effective problem-solving showed his ability to manage high-pressure situations creatively.
- **Strategic Thinking and Prioritization:** He identified immediate priorities while keeping long-term operational goals in focus.
- **Stakeholder Management:** His direct engagement with both internal teams and customers reflected strong collaboration and relationship-building skills.
- **Decisiveness and Confidence:** His actions under tight timelines demonstrated assured leadership and resilience.
- Team Empowerment: Setting up and leading a cross-functional crisis team illustrated his ability to empower and align diverse groups.
- **Result-Orientation and Accountability:** His focus on measurable results showcased his ownership and performance-driven mindset.
- **Communication Skills:** The structured and compelling manner in which he conveyed his story was itself evidence of strong executive communication—critical for any leadership role.

This reinforced a timeless truth in senior hiring: It's not enough to have experience—you must be able to articulate the same with structure, impact and authenticity.

## PREPARING FOR COMPETENCY-BASED QUESTIONS

To excel at competency-based interviews:

1. **Understand the Role:** Analyse the job description carefully to identify the core competencies being sought.
2. **Reflect on Past Experiences:** Create a bank of examples from professional, academic or extracurricular experiences demonstrating key competencies.
3. **Quantify Achievements:** Use metrics wherever possible. For instance, 'increased team efficiency by 20 per cent' is more powerful than 'improved efficiency'.
4. **Practise Mock Responses:** Rehearse answering questions aloud to build fluency and confidence.
5. **Seek Constructive Feedback:** Engage mentors or peers in mock interviews and fine-tune your responses based on their feedback.

### Sample Competency Questions and Model Answers

1. *Entrepreneurial Mindset*

**Question:** Tell me about a time you took an innovative approach to solve a problem.

**Answer (STAR):**

- **Situation:** As a project manager, our team faced declining client satisfaction due to delays.
- **Task:** My goal was to uncover root causes and propose improvements.

- **Action:** I implemented agile methodology, introduced task sprints, and set up a client feedback loop after each sprint.
- **Result:** Delivery timelines dropped by 30 per cent, and client satisfaction rose by 20 per cent within three months.

2. ***Empowering Teams***

   **Question:** Describe a time when you delegated tasks effectively.

   **Answer (STAR):**

   - **Situation:** During a product launch, overlapping team responsibilities led to delays.
   - **Task:** I needed to streamline roles and clarify ownership.
   - **Action:** I reorganized tasks based on strengths, assigned clear deliverables, and scheduled weekly check-ins.
   - **Result:** We completed the project two weeks early and exceeded launch sales targets by 15 per cent.

3. ***Building Partnerships***

   **Question:** Share an example of collaborating with stakeholders to achieve a goal.

   **Answer (STAR):**

   - **Situation:** I was part of a cross-functional team launching a new marketing campaign.
   - **Task:** Align sales, design and marketing teams with differing priorities.

- **Action:** I set up alignment meetings, created a shared roadmap, and mediated conflicts by emphasizing shared goals.
- **Result:** The campaign increased product awareness by 40 per cent and contributed to a 10 per cent revenue boost in the first quarter.

4. ***Demonstrating Resourcefulness***

**Question:** Provide an example of overcoming a significant resource constraint.

**Answer (STAR):**

- **Situation:** Our project budget was unexpectedly slashed by 25 per cent.
- **Task:** Deliver the project without compromising on quality.
- **Action:** I renegotiated vendor contracts, identified areas for scaling back, and adopted open-source tools.
- **Result:** The project was completed within budget while maintaining a 95 per cent client satisfaction score.

**Tips for Freshers Answering Competency-based Questions**

Freshers should draw examples from academic, internship, volunteering or leadership experiences:

- **Entrepreneurial Mindset:** Highlight initiatives taken during college projects.
- Empowering Teams: Share leadership experiences from group assignments.
- **Being Strategic:** Explain how you planned your

semester to balance academics, activities and personal goals.

**Building an Innings**

Think of competency-based interviews like building Test cricket innings.

You don't start by hitting every ball aggressively—you observe, adapt to the pitch, capitalize on loose balls, and build momentum steadily.

Similarly, in interviews, you must read the questions, adapt your examples smartly, and build your credibility story-by-story. Rushing into answers without structure is like throwing your wicket away early; crafting answers using STAR is like anchoring your innings toward a match-winning century.

## FINAL TAKEAWAY

Competency-based interviews are not about rattling off accomplishments; they are about illustrating who you are through authentic, structured storytelling.

When you prepare deeply, reflect honestly, and answer thoughtfully, you don't just participate in the interview—you control it. Whether you are a seasoned professional or a fresher, mastering competency-based questions positions you as a candidate ready not just to join an organization—but to elevate it.

## DEMONSTRATING COMPETENCE WITH CONTROL

**1. *Build Your Competency Bank***

Write two reusable STAR-based stories that clearly demonstrate your competencies.

**STAR Story 1:**

______________________________

**STAR Story 2:**

______________________________

*(These should work across multiple questions.)*

**2. *Competency Check***

Tick only if true for both stories:

- ☐ Situation and task are specific.
- ☐ Actions show *my* decisions and judgement.
- ☐ Results demonstrate impact (numbers or outcomes).

If any box is unchecked, the story lacks power.

**Key Reminder:** *Competency questions don't reward experience alone. They reward experience expressed with structure.*

# 12

## Navigating the Grey Area

In cricket, not every innings begins with boundaries. Sometimes, you walk in at 10 for 3 on a swinging pitch. It's murky and uncertain—a grey area.

Interviews often feel the same, especially when your resume carries baggage: short stints, a career break, or poor academics.

But grey doesn't mean weak. It means *human.*

How you bat through these grey patches—how you explain detours and stumbles—says more about your character, which matters the most.

### WHAT THE INTERVIEWER DOESN'T SAY ALOUD

A CV is rarely judged in isolation. Interviewers are scanning for reliability, self-awareness, and the ability to adapt. Grey areas raise unspoken questions:

- Did the candidate quit too quickly?
- Whether the candidate was asked to leave?
- Is the candidate a flight risk?

Your job? Answer these questions before they are asked—honestly, clearly and confidently.

## UNDERSTANDING THE GREY ZONE

These are the parts of your journey that don't look perfect on paper:

- Frequent job changes
- Career breaks or sabbaticals
- Demotions
- Poor academic records
- Industry or domain switch
- Entrepreneurship stints that didn't scale

Many walk into interviews feeling apologetic about these. The smarter ones? They walk in prepared—with insights, not excuses.

### The Rule of Honesty

Lying is never the answer. It risks inconsistencies, credibility loss or worse—disqualification.

But honesty doesn't mean oversharing or sounding regretful. It means framing the truth around growth, values and learning.

### Job-Hopping: Call It Course Correction

To interviewers, job-hopping can imply instability. To you, it might reflect exploration or organizational disruption.

#### *Example 1: Role Confusion*

In 2015, I left a job within nine months. I was hired to replace someone who was never removed. That created role overlap, team confusion and union issues.

**How I say it:**

'*There was a lack of role clarity, which affected my ability to contribute meaningfully. I value structured roles, so I moved on when a better-aligned opportunity arose.*'

***Example 2: Post-Merger Realignment***

I joined a steel company with long-term plans. But a merger led to demotion across the board, not just for me, which led to a short stint.

**How I say it:**

'*Post-merger, my role was realigned. While I understood the rationale, it no longer matched my aspirations. I chose to pursue roles where I could contribute more meaningfully.*'

Both responses are calm, rational and forward-looking.

**Career Breaks: Explain, Don't Apologize**

Breaks are not career crimes. They just need context.

- **Caregiving:** '*I paused to care for a family member. It was a demanding phase, but I gained resilience and perspective.*'
- **Health:** '*I had a brief health setback. I focused on recovery and am now fully recharged.*'
- **Exploration:** '*I took time to reassess my path. During this period, I completed a certification in supply-chain analytics, which clarified my next step.*'

## FRESHERS: TRIAL AND ERROR IS NATURAL

Changing courses, internships or even goals isn't a flaw—it's *career prototyping.*

- *'I tried marketing and consulting internships, but eventually discovered my affinity for product management. That trial clarified my focus.'*
- *'I shifted from commerce to human resources because I realized I am more inclined toward people strategy than number crunching.'*

Hiring managers appreciate clarity.

**Poor Academics: Shine a Light on the Turnaround**

Everyone loves a comeback.

- *'My early scores were low as I was focused on cricket, but when I decided to shift paths, I committed fully. I topped my postgrad diploma class.'*
- *'First-year engineering was overwhelming, but I developed a time-management system by second year that I still use today.'*
- *'Earlier, I was chasing my dream of becoming an actor or cricketer, and my academics suffered. But that phase taught me discipline, and once I pivoted, I applied that learning to my career.'*

Don't defend the dip. Highlight the climb.

**Demotions or Transfers: Be Candid, Not Defensive**

- *'Post-restructuring, I accepted a supporting role to retain continuity for the team. But I wanted more challenge, so I began exploring external options.'*
- *'I was moved to a less strategic position after the leadership changed. I stayed six months, contributed sincerely, and then transitioned respectfully.'*

## BUILDING YOUR GREY AREA NARRATIVE: A PRACTICE TEMPLATE

Here's a simple 4-part formula to craft any red-flag response:

> Acknowledge → Give context → Share the learning → Show readiness

Practise your narrative aloud. Write it down. Sharpen it. Your narrative should feel real, not rehearsed.

**Frame It like a Leader**

| Grey Area | Strong Framing Statement |
|---|---|
| Frequent job switches | *'Each move taught me what kind of environment I thrive in. I now know exactly what I'm looking for.'* |
| Career gap | *'The break helped me reset and refocus. I used it to build skills and return stronger.'* |
| Demotion/Role change | *'The new structure wasn't aligned with my strengths. I stayed professional and then sought a better fit.'* |
| Poor academics | *'I struggled with academics early on due to a lack of focus, but the experience taught me the importance of discipline. Since then, I have proven my abilities through strong, consistent real-world performance.'* |

## GREY AREAS IN LEADERSHIP

Grey zones don't disappear as you grow—they just shift shape.

A plant HR head who faced a lockout. A sales leader who missed quarterly targets due to market crashes. A CEO whose pivot flopped.

Even at the top, careers include missteps, misjudgements and misunderstood intentions.

The difference? Leaders learn to own outcomes—without excuses, but also without shame.

Whether you are a fresher or a functional head, grey areas don't disqualify you. But hiding them might.

**What Interviewers Actually Want to Know**

They are not testing your past—they are evaluating your *present mindset.*

- Have you reflected?
- Do you own your decisions?
- Are you resilient or reactive?
- Will you bring consistency now?

Grey areas test your clarity, maturity and honesty—not your eligibility.

**Questions to Ask Yourself before the Interview**

- What's the single most important thing I learned from this setback?
- How did this grey area shape my values or work ethic?
- If I had to explain this in one sentence, how would I say it without sounding defensive?

- Would I hire someone with this same story? If yes, why?

The goal isn't to create a cover story. It's to discover your *core story.*

**Final Batting Tips: How to Play the Tough Deliveries**

- Don't lie. It's a hit wicket.
- Don't blame. It's poor form.
- Don't ramble. Stay concise.
- Do frame it with insight.
- Do end with what you *bring now.*

## CLOSING THOUGHTS: YOUR GREY IS YOUR GROWTH

Cricket has room for gritty 30s, patient rebuilding, and glorious centuries. So does your career.

An interview isn't a court. It's a chance to show who you have become—not just what you have done.

So, walk in—not as someone hiding scars but as someone who's *earned stripes.*

Every grey patch is a prelude to your next innings. And when framed well, it won't be seen as a warning.

It will be seen as wisdom. And that's always worth *investing* in.

# 13

# How to Frame Your Salary Expectations

Cricket isn't just a game of boundaries—it's a game of timing, judgement and knowing when to play the right shot. Discussing salary in an interview is similar. It's not about making a bold statement or staying silent—it's about playing the right delivery with control and confidence.

Salary discussions are often the most anticipated and yet the most awkward phase of an interview. For candidates, it's a mix of excitement and anxiety. For employers, it's about balancing budgets with attracting and retaining talent. Like a tense run chase, this part of the conversation demands preparation, precision and emotional intelligence.

Let me start with a personal admission: I am not a compensation expert. In fact, when it comes to negotiating my own salary, I have often stumbled. My moves across roles weren't driven by pay hikes but by growth, values and learning. Yet, as an HR head, I have navigated countless salary negotiations for others—in the process, I have learned what truly works.

## THE COMMON PITFALLS: WHAT NOT TO DO

Most candidates trip up on the salary question because they either overshoot or undersell.

### 1. *The 'Unrealistic Ask' Trap*

Quoting an unreasonably high number without rationale is a common blunder. Confidence is important—but so is context. Most companies operate within defined salary bands. Unless you are bringing game-changing skills, going far beyond those bands can rule you out early.

### 2. *The 'Leave It to You' Surrender*

At the other end of the spectrum is surrender—'*I leave it to you*' or '*Anything as per your policy is fine*.' While this may seem humble, it often signals desperation, lack of market awareness, or confusion about self-worth. Worse, it can lead to lowball offers or even outright rejection.

### The Golden Rule: Be Honest, Be Clear

Inflating your current salary in hopes of boosting the offer might seem harmless—but it's risky. Background checks, HR networks, and payroll verification can expose discrepancies. And even if you sneak past, the breach of trust can shadow your credibility.

Instead of inflating figures, amplify your value. Talk about what you bring to the table—skills, outcomes, mindset. Build your case on performance, not fiction.

### Before the Interview: Prepare like a Pro

Just as a batter studies the pitch and the bowlers before going out, you must walk into salary discussions with insight and strategy.

**1.** ***Know the Role, Know the Market***

Use tools like Glassdoor, PayScale, and LinkedIn Salary Insights to understand market trends for your profile. Most companies aim to offer around the fiftieth–sixtieth percentile of the market—rarely more. Anchor your expectations accordingly.

**2.** ***Gauge the Employer's Range***

If a recruiter or consultant approaches you, try to learn the budget early. If it isn't disclosed, research the organization's pay philosophy, industry position and reviews. This helps you pitch realistically.

**3.** ***Break Down Your Own CTC***

Dissect your compensation—fixed, variable, ESOPs, benefits. Know what's negotiable and what isn't. This clarity can help you ask for a raise without appearing vague.

**4.** ***Know Your Priorities***

Ask yourself: Is salary my main driver—or is it learning, flexibility, brand or role maturity? A good offer aligns not just with your bank balance but also your purpose.

**How to Ask for a Hike without Losing the Deal**

A 20 per cent hike is standard—but there are no guarantees. What matters is how you position your ask.

**1.** ***Back It with Impact***

Use performance data, certifications and project outcomes to justify your value.

**Example:**

- 'I led a cost-optimization drive that saved INR 15 lakh annually.'
- 'My domain expertise helped onboard two key clients.'

The more measurable your pitch, the more credible it becomes.

**2. *Be Assertive, Not Aggressive***

Tone matters. Instead of saying *'I expect 50 per cent'*, try:

*'Based on my experience and the responsibilities outlined, I feel a range between X–Y would be fair.'*

**3. *Stay Open to the Full Picture***

Sometimes, brand equity, leadership exposure or cross-functional roles compensate for a modest hike. Evaluate the offer holistically. Don't miss out on a long-term win chasing short-term gains.

## HANDLING THE QUESTION: 'WHAT ARE YOUR SALARY EXPECTATIONS?'

Like a well-placed cover drive, your response must be timed and measured.

***If You Know the Budget:***

*'Based on my research and the scope of this role, I would expect something in the range of INR X to INR Y.'*

***If You Don't Know the Budget:***

Redirect thoughtfully:

- *'I would prefer to understand the company's compensation structure and how this role is positioned before quoting a figure.'*

Or offer a range with context:

- *'For roles of this nature in our industry, I have seen a typical range of INR X to Y. But I am open to discussing this based on the role specifics.'*

**Avoiding Desperation: Stay Grounded, Stay Professional**

Even if you really want the job, desperation weakens your hand.

***Do:***

- Express interest with confidence.
- Share how the company's values resonate with you.
- Keep your tone warm, yet businesslike.

***Don't:***

- Say, *'I'll take whatever you offer.'*
- Accept without reviewing.
- Sound overeager or impatient.

## BEYOND THE CTC: EVALUATE THE WHOLE OFFER

Salary is important—but it's just one part. Consider:

- Health insurance and wellness programmes

- Retirement benefits
- Learning and development opportunities
- Stock options or variable bonuses
- Culture, flexibility and growth

Sometimes, the best long-term payoff comes from roles that offer more than just money.

**When to Say No**

If the offer doesn't reflect your worth or long-term goals, it's okay to walk away.

You should reconsider the role if:

- The offer is significantly below market norms.
- There's little transparency or flexibility.
- The role doesn't align with your aspirations.

Turning down an offer is not rejection—it's redirection.

**Transactional Rewards vs Relational Rewards: Know What Truly Matters to You**

Before wrapping up your salary discussion or deciding on an offer, pause and reflect. Compensation is not just about money—it's about what matters most to you at this point in life.

Here are some key considerations worth reflecting on:

***Transactional Rewards (Tangible and Monetary):***

These directly impact your financial well-being and short-term goals.

- Base salary and fixed pay
- Performance-linked bonuses
- Joining/retention bonuses

- Stock options or ESOPs
- Provident fund, insurance, gratuity, etc.

***Relational Rewards (Intangible and Experiential):***

These shape your daily work life, emotional connection and long-term fulfilment.

- Work-Life balance and flexibility
- Supportive leadership and team culture
- Opportunities for learning and upskilling
- Brand prestige and professional credibility
- Job security and alignment with personal values

***Ask Yourself:***

- Am I seeking fast financial growth or long-term career development?
- Would I trade a higher salary for better hours or a healthier workplace?
- Does the company's mission and leadership inspire me?
- Is this role a means to an end or part of a larger journey?

There's no one-size-fits-all answer. Your definition of 'worth' must reflect where you are in your career, your responsibilities and your aspirations.

## FINAL WORD: TREAT IT LIKE A PARTNERSHIP, NOT A BARGAIN

Salary discussions aren't a game of one-upmanship. They're about mutual value creation. Show that you have done your homework, that you respect the company's constraints, and that you're here not just to earn—but to contribute.

Negotiate like a professional. Play the right shots. Time them well.

And remember, the goal isn't just to get the highest number—it's to find the right pitch to grow your career innings.

# 14

## The Final Question That Counts

In cricket, even when a team has posted a good total, the last over still matters. The final six balls are not just about adding a few runs—they're about consolidating the scoreboard, and finishing on a high.

The same applies to interviews.

After an intense exchange of questions and answers, when the energy begins to dip and the end seems near, the interviewer turns the tables and asks: '*Do you have any questions for us?*'

It sounds harmless—perhaps even a polite way to close the interaction. But make no mistake: this is your final over. How you handle it can consolidate your spot in the team and leave your innings on a high.

### WHY CANDIDATES MISS THIS GOLDEN OPPORTUNITY

Surprisingly, many candidates respond with a simple '*No*.' Some smile sheepishly. Others assume that the interview has already gone well and they would rather not ruin it with a misstep.

But here's what often causes that moment to slip away:

1. ***Nervousness and Fatigue***

Just like a cricketer drained by a long innings might falter in the last few overs, candidates—mentally taxed—may rush to the finish line, skipping what's actually a scoring opportunity.

2. ***Misreading the Moment***

Candidates often think, '*If they liked me, this won't matter*', but this moment offers a silent test. Silence here doesn't suggest confidence—it hints at indifference.

3. ***Lack of Preparation***

No matter how well you have performed until now, walking into the final question unprepared can expose a gap. And often, that's how promising interviews fall short—for missing the opportunity to reinforce your value when it matters most.

## WHY THIS QUESTION MATTERS

This isn't a formality. It's a window—your moment to flip the narrative, display strategic thinking, and engage with the interviewer as a peer.

Here's what interviewers are actually evaluating:

- **Interest in the Role:** Are you invested in the details, or just here for the ride?
- **Curiosity and Insight:** Can you think critically, connect dots, and ask what matters?
- **Cultural Fit:** Are you trying to understand the team, the manager, the working style?

In other words, the final question isn't about asking—it's about engaging.

**What to Ask: Making Every Question Count**

Not all questions are equal. The best ones are thoughtful, tailored and relevant. Just as a batsman doesn't play every ball the same way, you must adjust based on the match situation.

Here are five powerful types of questions you can use:

**1. *Role-specific Questions***

These reflect your focus on execution and success from day one.

- *'What does success look like in the first six months?'*
- *'What are the immediate challenges this role is expected to address?'*
- *'How will my performance be measured?'*

**Why it works:** It shows you're serious about the scoreboard and understand your KPIs before stepping in.

**2. *Team and Collaboration Questions***

Fit matters. So does chemistry with your squad.

- *'Can you share more about the team I would be part of?'*
- *'How does this team typically collaborate across functions?'*
- *'What's the leadership style of the reporting manager?'*

**Why it works:** It signals that you want to contribute—not just perform. That you are thinking beyond your bat.

**3. *Company-specific Questions***

These reveal you've studied the pitch—and the stadium.

- *'I read about your expansion into [X market]—how does that shape this department?'*
- *'What defines your company culture?'*
- *'How do you nurture internal talent for future roles?'*

**Why it works:** It reflects that you've done your homework, and you're here for more than a pay cheque.

**4. *Business Strategy Questions***

Particularly for experienced professionals, these questions signal leadership thinking.

- *'How does this role contribute to your long-term strategic priorities?'*
- *'What market shifts are you preparing for over the next two to three years?'*
- *'How do you define success beyond numbers?'*

**Why it works:** You come across not just as a player, but a captain in the making.

**5. *Personalized Questions for the Interviewer***

A touch of rapport can humanize the conversation.

- *'What do you enjoy most about working here?'*
- *'How has your journey evolved within the company?'*
- *'What would you say defines success here beyond performance?'*

**Why it works:** You build connection. You show that you're evaluating the team as much as they are evaluating you.

## The Questions You Should Not Ask

Every batter knows what not to attempt on a tricky pitch. Similarly, avoid these pitfalls:

### 1. *Compensation-First Questions*

Asking, '*What's the salary range?*' before they're ready to offer, shows you're batting for money, not the match.

Instead, let your value shine. The right time for negotiations is after you are selected.

### 2. *Questions Easily Answered by Google*

Never ask, '*What does your company do?*' You'll sound like someone who didn't even check the scoreboard.

### 3. *Confrontational Questions*

If you want to ask about challenges, phrase them wisely: Instead of, '*Why has your market share declined?*' ask, '*How is the team responding to shifts in market dynamics?*'

### 4. *Too Many Questions*

Always remember: quality over quantity. One to two solid questions are enough—unless you are invited to continue.

## Preparing for the Moment: Pre-Match Practice

Just like a batsman visualizes deliveries before facing them, you should plan your questions in advance.

### 1. *Study the Job and the Company*

Use LinkedIn, company reports and news articles. Know their business like you know your stats.

**2. *Customize to the Interviewer***

If it's the hiring manager—ask about the role. If it's HR—ask about culture or career pathing.

**3. *Rehearse the Delivery***

Questions aren't meant to be read out mechanically. Practise so they feel authentic and confident.

## HOW ASKING QUESTIONS BENEFITS YOU TOO

An interview isn't a one-way assessment—it's a conversation between two decision-makers. Just as the company is evaluating your fit, you are assessing whether this role, this culture and this leadership will support your growth and aspirations.

Here's how asking the right questions serves your own clarity:

- ***Brings Role Clarity***
  Understand the real expectations behind the job description. What outcomes will define success in this role?

- ***Tests Cultural Alignment***
  Every company claims a great culture. Your questions help you discover whether their values are practised or just printed.

- ***Reveals Growth Opportunities***
  Get a clearer picture of how the company invests in learning, promotions and internal mobility. Are you joining a place where you can build a long innings?

- ***Surfaces Leadership Style***
  The manager you report to often shapes your experience more than the organization. Your queries can subtly unearth how they lead, support and empower.

- ***Strengthens Decision-making***
  The interview is not just about getting selected—it's about choosing wisely. The insights you gather will help you decide if this is the right platform for your next career move.

## FINAL THOUGHTS: OWN YOUR LAST OVER

When the interviewer says, '*Do you have any questions for us?*' don't see it as the end.

See it as your chance to:

- Leave a lasting impression.
- Show maturity and strategy.
- Demonstrate curiosity, not desperation.

Because interviews, like matches, are rarely won in the first over alone. Sometimes, it's your last shot that clinches the victory.

And the ones who ask well—they don't just get selected. They get remembered.

Just as importantly, asking the right questions gives *you* the clarity to decide whether this is the right field to play your next innings.

# 15

# Harnessing Knowledge: Your Path to Influence

In cricket, technique is your foundation. In your career, knowledge plays the same role. It's not just a source of strength—it's your positioning, your advantage, your identity.

It speaks on your behalf—sometimes louder than your words. And in interviews, it quietly but powerfully tells the interviewer that this individual comes prepared.

## WHY KNOWLEDGE MATTERS MORE THAN EVER

It need not be overemphasized—as professionals, companies look primarily at your domain knowledge and the expertise you bring in your chosen field. That is one of the key reasons they invest in you. Whether you're just entering the corporate world or have been navigating it for decades, your domain expertise can be a decisive factor. It conveys maturity, credibility and readiness—qualities that cannot be faked.

### From Theory to Application: The Real Interview Currency

Many candidates believe that recalling textbook information will get them through an interview. But interviews aren't memory tests—they're reality checks.

It's not about what you know; it's about how well you understand it and how effectively you can apply it. That's where most candidates struggle—they either fail to go beyond surface-level understanding or can't explain the practical relevance of what they've learned.

Whether you are a fresher (where clarity of fundamentals is key) or an experienced professional (where the depth of application matters), your ability to think critically and communicate insights clearly is what separates you from the rest.

The moment you begin to demonstrate this, the interview evolves. You are no longer being evaluated—you are being engaged. You are seen not as a job seeker, but as a problem-solver.

## Building a Strong Knowledge Base: Start Early, Stay Curious

The best time to build your knowledge was yesterday. The second-best time is today.

***Action Tips:***

- If you are a fresher—your knowledge and conceptual clarity will be tested. If you are experienced, ensure you possess both theoretical and practical application knowledge—and be prepared to demonstrate it.
- Don't stop at academic material—read industry blogs, business dailies and thought pieces in your domain area.
- Follow leading voices in your field on LinkedIn or Twitter.
- Subscribe to relevant podcasts, journals and newsletters in your field.

## My Journey: From Below Average to Ahead of the Curve

When I began my professional journey, I wasn't among the academic toppers. A few interviews I attended made me realize that I lacked a strong foundation in my domain.

I went back to my textbooks with renewed intent, this time focusing on concepts I had earlier skimmed through. I began reading more, taking notes and learning from industry veterans. In our time, we didn't have the luxury of social media.

Another unconventional—but effective—learning tool I found was interviews.

I would record every question asked, go home, research the answers, and strengthen my grasp. Over time, this habit helped me build a rich personal repository of questions and tailored responses.

Keeping a journal of my interview experiences proved invaluable for future interviews. It allowed me to:

- Spot patterns in questions.
- Anticipate what would be asked next.
- Identify where I struggled and why.
- Refine my responses with each experience.

One of my mentors once told me:

*'Never turn down an interview. You don't have to accept the job—but every interview gives you a sense of how the world perceives your worth.'*

Interviews can be excellent rehearsal rooms, strategic checkpoints and platforms for self-assessment.

## ADDRESSING WEAK SPOTS: A SIGN OF STRENGTH, NOT DEFICIENCY

Even after years in the industry, I have never believed in becoming too comfortable.

Not long ago, I enrolled in an HR certification programme at XLRI—not to embellish my resume, but to deepen my understanding in an area I felt needed reinforcement. The course demanded time, financial investment and effort. But the insights it offered were invaluable.

**Lesson:** Acknowledging your knowledge gaps doesn't weaken your image—it strengthens your intent.

### Play to Your Strengths: Steer the Game Your Way

Every professional has a domain or sub-domain in which they excel.

During interviews, learn to subtly steer the conversation in that direction—not forcefully, but naturally—by picking up cues and building on them. I call these moments 'loose balls'—opportunities where you can demonstrate depth.

If you sense the discussion entering your area of comfort, seize it. Share experiences. Offer thoughtful solutions. Articulate your expertise with clarity.

Often, I've seen interviewers skip over my weaker areas—not because they overlooked them, but because the depth of the discussion in my area of strength gave them what they needed. Sometimes, they might even be facing similar challenges themselves and want to hear your perspective.

That's the power of playing to your strengths. You shift the momentum of the interview—and take control of the narrative.

**Stay Updated: Professional Security over Job Security**

In a world that changes rapidly, yesterday's knowledge quickly becomes outdated.

That's why staying relevant is not optional—it's essential.

***What Helps to Stay Current:***

- Reading for at least 30 minutes daily in your domain—make this a habit.
- Subscribing to domain-specific magazines and updates.
- Attending webinars, workshops and panel discussions.
- Following industry leaders and engaging in online communities.
- Staying connected with peers and professionals in your field.
- Also, when you share your learning—whether by mentoring juniors, posting on LinkedIn, or speaking in discussions—you not only contribute, but deepen your own understanding.

If you keep learning, you remain employable—and that's the best kind of career insurance.

**Turn Knowledge into Interview Advantage**

Knowledge isn't for display—it's a tool to solve, to influence, to connect.

In interviews, here's how to use it effectively:

- **Do Your Homework:** Understand the company's market, culture and key challenges.

- **Tell Stories, Not Just Facts:** Use real-life examples to bring your responses to life.
- **Be Thorough in Your Area:**
  - For freshers, clarity on basics is crucial.
  - For experienced professionals, support your expertise with real examples and measurable outcomes.

Every interviewer is silently evaluating: *Can this person add value?* Your clarity and depth of knowledge is the best proof.

## CLOSING THOUGHTS: LET KNOWLEDGE SPEAK LOUDEST

With strong domain knowledge, you walk into an interview not with anxiety but assurance. It gives you the clarity to speak with purpose and the confidence to engage as an equal.

In the professional world, confidence rooted in expertise stands tall—while credentials without substance often crumble.

***Knowledge:***

- Builds your personal brand
- Wins trust
- Solves problems
- Inspires followership

You don't need to be the loudest in the room. If you speak with substance and provide the answers the interviewer is seeking, people will listen.

So, wherever you are on your journey—entry-level or executive—make knowledge your most powerful ally. Read, reflect, learn and apply.

Because in this game, knowledge is not just your bat; it's your helmet, pads, gloves—your entire kit.

# 16

# Making Your Word Count: The Power of Communication

In an age where competition is intensifying, the ability to express yourself clearly isn't just helpful—it's non-negotiable.

Interviews don't just assess what you've done. They assess how you think. And the fastest way to demonstrate your thinking? Through how you communicate.

**Clarity is credibility. Confidence is currency.**

Let's be clear: Speaking well doesn't mean speaking in English alone. It means speaking with structure, purpose and intention regardless of language. But for many professional roles, English is often the common medium. And in that space, fluency isn't about fancy words—it's about precise ones.

## COMMUNICATION IS A WINDOW INTO YOUR MIND

What we say—and how we say it—reveals how we think. The ability to convey your thoughts with purpose and structure tells interviewers that you can also lead meetings, navigate conflict, explain ideas and influence people.

Let's be clear: language is only the surface. Communication is the real skill.

### The Interview Is a Conversation, Not a Performance

A common misconception is that interviews are oral exams—that you must get every word right. This belief fuels anxiety and memorized responses.

But great interviews are not perfect performances. They are persuasive conversations.

And like all good conversations, they require you to:

- Listen deeply
- Speak deliberately
- Connect authentically

When your communication style feels rehearsed or robotic, it creates distance. When it feels grounded, conversational and thoughtful, it builds trust.

### Three Types of Communicators and Who Gets Hired

1. ***The Over-Polished Performer***
   They speak in flawless grammar. But every sentence sounds memorized. They are hard to connect with. The conversation feels cold and calculated.

2. ***The Underprepared Wanderer***
   They have strong intent but ramble. They jump between thoughts. Their passion is buried under poor delivery. Their answers lack closure.

3. ***The Structured Storyteller***
   They speak with warmth and clarity. They structure answers with a beginning, middle and end. They are not flawless but they are fluent in their own truth.

**Guess who gets the job?**

The third one. Every time.

## STRUCTURE: THE BACKBONE OF STRONG COMMUNICATION

You don't need perfect English. You need organized thinking.

One of the simplest ways to sound coherent in an interview is to use frameworks. These frameworks help you think before you speak—and that's what interviewers are really listening for.

Different questions demand different structures:

- **STAR** (Situation, Task, Action, Result): For experience-based answers
- **PREP** (Point, Reason, Example, Point): For opinion- and judgement-based questions
- **Pause and Pivot:** When you need a moment to gather your thoughts before responding

Communication improves not by memorizing better sentences, but by organizing better thoughts.

### PREP

While STAR works best when describing past experiences, interviews also test how you think, not just what you've done. Questions that begin with 'What do you think…', 'Do you believe…', or 'How would you…' are best handled using PREP.

**PREP** stands for:

- P – Point: State your view clearly
- R – Reason: Explain why you think so
- E – Example: Support it with logic or a brief example
- P – Point (Reiterate): Reinforce your message

**Live PREP Interview Example**

**Interview Question:** *Do you believe unions help or hinder business performance?*

**Answer using PREP:**

- **Point:** I believe unions, when engaged constructively, help business performance rather than hinder it.
- **Reason:** They provide a formal channel for employee voice, help manage workplace expectations, and contribute to industrial stability when relationships are based on trust and dialogue.
- **Example:** In one of my assignments, regular engagement with the union helped us resolve issues early, avoid disruptions, and implement productivity linked initiatives with employee buy-in.
- **Point** (Reiterate): So, while adversarial relationships can create challenges, constructive union engagement ultimately supports sustainable business performance.

**Real Story: Manoj Kumar Sharma (from *12th Fail*)— Simplicity, Structure and Sincerity in Communication**

In *12th Fail*, the biographical story of IPS officer Manoj Kumar Sharma, one of the most defining moments comes during his UPSC Civil Services interview. After years of struggle—

poverty, social ridicule and academic setbacks—Manoj sits before the panel that will decide his future.

He chooses to speak in Hindi, his most comfortable language. But more importantly, he speaks with:

- Flawless structure
- Measured tone
- Genuine conviction
- Steady eye contact

When asked tough, situation-based questions, Manoj doesn't try to please. He doesn't fumble or get theatrical. He remains composed, transparent and thoughtful.

There's no performance. No ornamental English. Just a grounded candidate communicating with clarity and sincerity.

His responses reflect all three key communication tools:

- STAR for experiential questions.
- PREP for opinion-based answers.
- Pause and Pivot when unsure; he takes a moment to gather his thoughts, then replies with intent.

And that's how he clears the interview—not because he spoke the Queen's English, but because he communicated like a future officer.

**Beyond Words: The Four Signals You're Always Sending**

Even before you speak, you are already communicating through non-verbal cues. Here's what you need to know:

1. ***Posture Speaks before You Do***

- Sit upright without stiffness

- Keep your shoulders open and relaxed
- Don't fold your arms—it signals resistance
- Don't fidget—it signals nervous energy

Interviewers read your posture the way a pilot reads cockpit instruments.

2. ***Eye Contact Builds Micro Trust***

- Look at the interviewer(s) when speaking, without staring
- Shift gaze gently across a panel if present
- Avoid looking down while answering—it breaks connection

Eye contact isn't about dominance. It's about engagement.

3. ***Facial Expressions Add Texture***

A flat face, even with perfect answers, feels lifeless.

- Smile occasionally (but don't fake it)
- Nod to show comprehension
- React when appropriate—it shows you are present

Emotions, when expressed genuinely, make your answers stick.

4. ***Gestures Give Life to Your Words***

- Use your hands to emphasize points, not to distract
- Keep movements measured and open
- Avoid hiding hands under the table—they convey defensiveness

Communication is choreography. It's how your voice and body align.

### English vs Vernacular: What Really Matters

Let's be practical: in many roles—client-facing, leadership, management, law, consulting—English proficiency is expected. It helps navigate multi-cultural workplaces, draft reports, lead presentations.

But English isn't a measure of intelligence or capability.

In numerous functional, shop-floor, field or grassroots roles, what matters more is **clarity of thought and relevance of communication**, not the language you speak in.

### What Should Guide You?

- If the panel seems comfortable in a local language, and the role allows, seek permission and switch.
- Always be respectful: '*Would you be okay if I explain this in Bengali/Hindi?*'
- Never switch because of panic—switch because it will help communicate better.

**Remember:** Language is a medium. Communication is the message.

### Your 5-point Communication Drill before Any Interview

1. **Record yourself** answering common questions. Review posture, tone, pace and expression.
2. **Practise with feedback.** Get a mentor or peer to evaluate not just your content but your delivery, especially if you are a fresher.
3. **Slow down.** Most candidates rush. The best ones pause.
4. **Speak with intention, not fear.** Don't dilute your message by over-explaining.

5. **End your answers cleanly.** No 'so yeah...', 'that's it...', 'I guess...' Close with confidence.

## LISTENING IS ALSO COMMUNICATION

Sometimes, the most powerful thing you can do in an interview is not speak but listen.

There are interviewers who talk more than they ask. They elaborate questions, offer their own views, or even answer the question halfway themselves. They are like the famous news anchor you know—full of commentary, sometimes forgetting they are the one conducting the interview.

With such interviewers, your job becomes easier. Let them speak. Let them explain.

Listen actively. Nod at the right moments. Make them feel heard. Then insert your insight. Don't interrupt. Don't overcompensate. Just add a thoughtful point and step back.

In communication, silence—used wisely—is strength. This kind of listening builds trust.

## FINAL THOUGHT: SPEAK TO BE REMEMBERED

You don't need a silver tongue. You need a clear voice, a grounded tone, and a well-structured message.

Interviews are not about linguistic perfection. They're about alignment, expression and impression.

When you communicate with calm energy, structured responses and human warmth, the interview doesn't feel like a test. It feels like a partnership taking shape.

And that's how offers are made.

# 17

# Interview Etiquette and Body Language: A Winning Combination

Interviews begin long before the first question is asked. The moment you enter the room—whether physical or virtual—you are being assessed.

Not just for your qualifications, but for your presence, preparedness and professionalism.

How you dress, how you wait, how you greet—these cues shape the first impression before you even speak.

In interviews, etiquette is not optional. It is your silent way of saying:

'*I value this opportunity and have come prepared to earn it.*'

## FIRST IMPRESSIONS ARE NOT COSMETIC—THEY ARE CONTEXTUAL

In professional settings, attire and grooming are not superficial—they are signifiers of seriousness.

Think of a courtroom. A lawyer walks in wearing jeans and a t-shirt. Regardless of their legal acumen, the judge forms an instant perception: They are not serious about the setting.

The same applies to interviews.

You may be the best fit on paper but if your presence doesn't reflect preparation, you start with a disadvantage.

### The Blazer I Forgot

Two years ago, I was scheduled for a final interview with the managing director of a reputed firm.

I was confident. I had prepared thoroughly. But I did not wear one essential item—my blazer.

When I entered the CHRO's cabin (who had already interviewed me earlier), he asked bluntly:

'Where is your blazer?'

'*I haven't come with it*,' I replied.

His response was sharper than I expected:

'Do you realize this is an interview with the MD? Does that mean you're not taking it seriously?'

That comment stayed with me. Though I cracked that interview, I learned my lesson.

Before your answers, your appearance does the talking.

### Dressing Right: Not a Trend, but a Tribute

In recent years, many candidates—particularly from the younger generation—view formality as outdated.

But an interview isn't a casual catch-up. It's a ritual of evaluation.

Choosing to dress formally signals:

- That you value the opportunity.
- That you respect the interviewer's time.
- That you understand the occasion.

***For Men:***

- Suit or blazer (navy, black, grey) with a collared shirt
- Tie optional based on industry, but safe in most cases
- Polished formal shoes

***For Women:***

- Formal Western or Indian business attire
- Neat grooming, minimal accessories
- Professional footwear

**Virtual interviews?** Dress the same. Not just for appearance, but for mindset.

**Beyond Dress: The Subtle Art of Interview Decorum**

Etiquette is not just about clothes. It's the full orchestration of how you show up.

1. ***Punctuality***
   Arriving five minutes early isn't about the fear of missing the interview. It's about respecting the other person's time.

2. ***Your Wait Matters***
   Don't slump on the waiting-room couch, scroll endlessly, or look impatient. Even in reception areas, people are watching. Sit upright. Stay alert. Be composed.

3. ***Greeting Matters***
   A simple '*Good morning*' or '*Pleasure to meet you*' delivered with a calm smile sets the tone. Don't walk in without acknowledgement—or worse, without confidence.

4. ***Handle Documents Gracefully***

   If asked for your resume or portfolio, present it—don't toss it. Small gestures signal large intentions.

**Body Language: Presence without Words**

Your body speaks before your voice does.

In high-pressure environments like interviews, non-verbal cues are often more revealing than spoken ones.

- Sit upright, with open shoulders—not stiff, but alert.
- Avoid crossed arms or folded hands—they signal defensiveness.
- Keep hand movements minimal but natural—don't fidget.
- Make appropriate eye contact—not a stare, but a steady presence.
- Smile genuinely, not constantly—let it punctuate your words when needed.

In the absence of words, your posture, gestures and facial expressions silently narrate your mindset.

Body language isn't about acting; it's **about alignment between your inner confidence and outer presence**.

## PRESENCE IS PRACTICE

Imagine walking into the lobby of a star hotel.

You are not greeted by words alone—you are greeted by how the space feels:

- Clean floors
- Fresh fragrance

- Staff standing upright, attentive but not intrusive
- Lighting, temperature and tone—all curated

Now imagine another hotel—untidy reception, inattentive staff, dim lighting and no sense of welcome.

Which place earns your trust—even before you check in?

An interview room is no different.

Your posture, your attire, your calm demeanour—these become your lobby. They set the tone for everything that follows.

The best candidates understand this. They don't just walk in to answer questions—they walk in to represent their own 'brand'.

**Rapport Is Built on Respect, Not Overfamiliarity**

Candidates often misinterpret 'be yourself' to mean 'be casual'. But an interview is not a living-room chat.

While warmth and confidence are appreciated, etiquette helps you avoid:

- Interrupting the interviewer
- Overstepping with humour or informality
- Dominating a discussion

Adapt to the room. If the interviewer is formal, mirror that tone. If they warm up later, match their energy gradually.

Think of rapport not as an ice-breaker but as a bridge—earned, not assumed.

**Etiquette Signals Culture Fit**

Companies don't just hire for competence. They hire for compatibility.

Your behaviour in the interview is seen as a preview of how you will behave with:

- Clients
- Team members
- Leaders
- Cross-functional stakeholders

Good etiquette signals:

- You know how to represent the brand
- You will not be a cultural misfit
- You take pride in professionalism

## IN SUMMARY

1. **Dress the Role:** Your attire signals intent. Always dress one level above the role.
2. **Respect Time and Space:** Arrive early. Wait with composure. Carry yourself like a professional from the first second.
3. **Greet and Engage Thoughtfully:** A firm hello can speak louder than your resume.
4. **Match the Tone, Don't Manufacture It:** Let rapport build naturally, never forced.
5. **Carry Yourself as a Future Colleague:** Your etiquette is the lens through which they imagine working with you.

**Professionalism Is Not an Act—It's a Habit**

- Interview etiquette isn't about scripted behaviour—it reflects a mindset of respect.
- Your punctuality, attire, tone and composure signal how

seriously you take responsibility.

- These aren't finishing touches; they are foundational indicators of how you work.
- In high-stakes roles, trust is built through consistent, quiet discipline.
- Your qualifications may get you the interview—but your presence earns the confidence.
- Etiquette isn't performative; it's predictive.
- It shows how you will behave under pressure, represent the company, and uphold professionalism beyond the interview.

## FINAL THOUGHT: LET YOUR PRESENCE SPEAK BEFORE YOU DO

An interview begins before the first question and continues long after your last word.

Dress like it matters. Sit like you belong. Behave like you're ready.

Because when you walk in with presence and humility, the interviewer sees more than a candidate—they see a professional already prepared for the job.

# 18

# Stay Calm, Stay Confident: Your Path to Cracking Interviews

Let's admit it.

No matter how confident you are, the moment your name is called, your palms sweat a bit. The wait outside feels longer than it is, and once inside, it can feel like every word, every expression, every silence is under a microscope.

And that's completely natural.

But here's the truth: The interviewer isn't trying to trap you. Most are simply trying to find, among many questions, an answer to one:

'*Can this person handle pressure?*'

And the clearest way to show that you can is to stay calm and confident.

## WHY COMPOSURE MATTERS MORE THAN YOU THINK

Most people think interviews are all about content and communication. But in **reality your presence, energy, and steadiness** often leave a deeper impression.

Here's why:

- People remember calm energy, not just rehearsed answers.
- Composed candidates come across as dependable. Anxious ones feel risky.
- Confidence doesn't mean knowing everything. It means staying grounded even when you don't.

**What Calm Looks like**

It's not about being emotionless or robotic. Calmness is visible in small, intentional choices:

- Taking a normal breath before you respond
- Smiling naturally, even when the question is challenging
- Admitting what you don't know—with maturity
- Sitting with ease—not slouching, not frozen
- Speaking with clarity—not speed or flair

## 'BUT I STILL FEEL NERVOUS...'

That's completely normal. Nervousness is not your enemy.

What trips most candidates is not the *nerves* but how they *react* to them.

Trying to fight or bury your anxiety often makes it worse. The smarter response is to acknowledge it, breathe through it, and move forward despite it.

Here's how you can prepare your mind and body:

***Before the Interview:***

- Practise slow, deep breathing—inhale for four seconds, hold for four seconds, and exhale for six seconds; repeat thrice.

- Tell yourself—'*I am not here to impress. I am here to express.*'

***While Waiting:***

- Sit upright, shoulders relaxed.
- Smile gently, breathe normally.

***When You Enter:***

- Greet with warmth and composure.
- Don't rush to sit or unpack.
- Take a moment. Let your energy settle.

**Remember:** The interviewer is reading not just your resume but your rhythm.

**Everyday Calm: You've Done This Before**

Think about it.

You have walked into an exam room unsure of one answer.

You have stood on stage while your heart raced.

You have met someone important and forgotten your lines.

Yet, you carried on. You gathered yourself. You made it through.

An interview is no different.

It only feels bigger because we are told it's a 'make-or-break' moment. But it isn't. It's just another human conversation with slightly higher stakes.

**Take a relatable example:** Ever seen someone begin a speech with trembling hands, then find their flow after a few lines? That's nervous energy transitioning into control. Interviews follow the same curve. The first two minutes may feel shaky, but you will find your rhythm if you breathe, stay present, and treat it like a dialogue, not a test.

**The Interviewer Is Human Too**

Here's something most people overlook: The person on the other side of the table is human too.

Interviewers aren't superheroes. They have meetings, backlogs, and sometimes, even their own nervousness—especially when interviewing someone from a senior domain or a different field.

They are not trying to intimidate you. In fact, they are hoping you make their job easier—by being prepared, authentic and composed.

So, the next time you're in that chair, remind yourself: This isn't a courtroom; it's a conversation.

And the candidate who breathes before speaking, who doesn't panic after a pause, who listens fully before replying—that's the one who quietly stands out.

Because calmness isn't about never feeling pressure. It's about showing that you think clearly *under* pressure.

**Tactical Application: Calm in Action**

Just like a seasoned batter adjusts to each ball, you must adapt moment to moment.

- ***Opening Questions:***
  Start with a warm smile and steady tone. No need to rush.

- ***Tough or Unexpected Questions:***
  Pause. Think. Then respond.
  Use bridging phrases like:

- *'That's a good question—here's how I'd think about it.'*
- *'May I take a moment to consider that?'*

➤ ***Mistakes or Misspeaks:***

Own them with calm clarity:

*'Let me rephrase that to explain better.'*

*'That's something I am actively learning more about.'*

Interviewers don't expect perfection. But they respect presence of mind.

**When You Feel Overwhelmed Mid-Interview**

Even the best-prepared candidates can feel thrown off. When that happens:

- Focus on your breath.
- Politely ask for a moment or to revisit the question.
- Take a sip of water if available.
- Mentally reset: '*This is a conversation, not a test.*'

Remember: It's not about never stumbling. It's about how you recover.

The most successful candidates aren't flawless—they're resilient.

**You Deserve to Be in That Room**

Often, the biggest challenge isn't the interview—it's believing you belong there.

You may feel underqualified. You may come from a humble background. You may carry the weight of past rejections.

But remember: You got the call. That means they already saw something in you.

You didn't sneak into that room. You earned your seat.

Your job now isn't to prove your worth. It's to bring it alive—with clarity, presence and courage.

And if it doesn't go your way? You don't lose. You learn. You sharpen your edge.

Every successful career has chapters of 'almost', 'not yet', and 'close calls' right before the real breakthrough happens.

So, carry your calm like a badge. Wear your confidence with quiet pride.

Your best innings might be just one interview away.

## FINAL WORDS: CALM IS QUIET STRENGTH

Whether you're a fresher or a seasoned leader, the candidate who remains composed in the interview room communicates something powerful:

That you are steady.

That you are self-aware.

That you don't crack when the pressure mounts—you think.

Because calmness is not the absence of nerves. It's the ability to respond instead of react.

And confidence? It's not a performance. It's the quiet belief that you will find your footing, one question at a time.

So, walk in. Sit tall. Speak with intent. And remember: Your calm presence is often your loudest answer.

# 19

# Honesty Pays: Turning Transparency into Triumph

In sport, as in life, true character is shown when you choose honesty before being asked. Legends like Gavaskar and Tendulkar have walked off without waiting for the umpire because they knew they were out. That kind of self-awareness and integrity is what sets true professionals apart—whether on the field or in an interview. Similarly, in interviews, how you respond to difficult questions—especially those about gaps, failures or career stumbles—reveals more about your character than a flawless academic record ever could.

And nothing steadies the bat quite like honesty.

While many candidates believe interviews are about showcasing perfection, seasoned interviewers are scanning for something deeper—integrity, self-awareness and resilience. These qualities don't emerge from rehearsed responses. They shine through honest storytelling.

## THE HONEST INNINGS: WHERE IT BEGINS

Honesty in interviews doesn't start at the question. It starts long before you step into the room—with how you evaluate *yourself*.

Ask:

- Can I confidently explain my journey, including the ups and downs?
- Am I prepared to talk about challenges without being defensive?

This early self-check serves two purposes. It ensures that you apply only to roles that genuinely suit you, and it helps you enter interviews with calm confidence. When you're honest with yourself first, your responses come across as grounded and real. And that's exactly what interviewers notice.

**Owning My Grey Patches: A Straight-Bat Approach**

After the pandemic, my career had a rough patch. I switched jobs more frequently than usual—some roles ended sooner than expected while others simply didn't work out.

In one interview, the director pointed to the pattern: 'I see a few short stints during these periods.'

I responded: '*Yes, there were a few transitions that didn't go as planned. In fact, if I may add, there's another brief stint here that lasted only nine months.*'

That moment caught his attention. He appreciated that I had voluntarily highlighted something he might have missed. The tone of the conversation shifted. I was trusted for my honesty. Eventually, I got the job.

Being honest about those stints didn't make me look weak. It made me look confident, self-aware and dependable.

**Strategic Honesty: Your Edge in High-Stakes Conversations**

1. **It Builds Trust:** Interviewers are trained to detect evasion. A genuine response fosters credibility.

2. **It Differentiates You:** Most candidates aim to impress. Honest candidates aim to connect.
3. **It Reflects Maturity:** Owning your setbacks signals self-awareness and growth potential.
4. **It Converts Weakness into Strength:** When framed well, setbacks become stories of resilience, not red flags.

### Tackling Bouncers: How to Navigate Difficult Questions Honestly

Honesty doesn't mean baring every detail or sounding apologetic. It's about presenting the truth with clarity and control.

- **Acknowledge the Issue:** Don't sidestep. Own it.
- Provide Brief Context: Stick to the facts. Avoid blame or emotional justifications.
- **Highlight the Learning:** What did the experience teach you? What changed after?
- **Keep It Positive:** Stay composed, professional and forward-looking.

Think of it like handling a rising delivery: You don't flinch or swing wildly. You absorb it with a straight bat and measured timing.

## HONESTY AS YOUR INTERVIEW USP

In another interview, a senior level candidate was asked about a project that hadn't delivered the expected results. He didn't sugar-coat it. He explained what went wrong, the corrective steps he took, and how the experience shaped his approaches to risk management.

The panellists were impressed with his candour. Most people avoid failure stories. But he chose to be open and honest, and made the discussion insightful.

So, honesty doesn't just protect candidacy—it elevates it.

### What Happens when You Are Dishonest?

A fabricated answer may get you through an interview, but it creates long-term risk:

- **Loss of Trust:** A minor inconsistency can create doubt about everything else.
- **Damage to Reputation:** If the truth surfaces later, it can impact references, credibility or even your job.
- **Mental Fatigue:** Keeping track of half-truths adds pressure and affects performance.

Honesty is simpler, cleaner and far more sustainable.

### Beyond the Interview: Honesty as a Long-Term Advantage

The value of honesty goes far beyond clearing an interview. It shapes the kind of roles you land and the support you receive once you are in them.

In one of my earlier roles, I openly admitted during the interview that I lacked practical exposure in a specific domain. Instead of holding it against me, the hiring manager appreciated the candour and ensured I received hands-on training from day one. That learning experience ended up accelerating my growth.

Being honest early on helped set the right expectations, built immediate trust, and made me more coachable in the eyes of my team.

## EMBRACING HONESTY: A CAREER PHILOSOPHY, NOT A TACTIC

Just like a cricketer doesn't fake his form to make it to the playing 11, you shouldn't fake your narrative to get hired. Honesty isn't a temporary strategy—it's a long-term edge.

It shows that:

- You know yourself and your boundaries.
- You are confident enough to admit imperfections.
- You are open to learning, correction and growth.

Honest professionals are easier to mentor, promote and retain. And that's why organizations trust them more.

**Practical Nets: How to Train for Honest Interviews**

- **Self-reflect Often:** Understand your career patterns—successes, missteps and transitions.
- **Anticipate Tough Questions:** Prepare for them with clarity, not defensiveness.
- **Reframe, Don't Excuse:** Position your challenges as turning points, not regrets.
- **Seek Feedback:** Ask mentors or trusted colleagues how your narrative comes across.

Like a net practice before a big match, these habits ensure that your real stories are interview-ready.

## FINAL WORDS: HONESTY ALWAYS PAYS

In a world full of defensive strokes and fake cover drives, authenticity hits different. It's not just about getting selected—

it's about walking into the team as your best self.

Interviewers may forget numbers, frameworks or tools you mention. But they will remember how you made them feel—especially if you spoke with courage, clarity and conviction.

So, the next time you are asked about a difficult chapter in your journey, don't duck the ball. Stand tall, play it straight, and trust your timing.

Because in the game of interviews—as in cricket—the straight bat of honesty often scores the most meaningful runs.

**QUIET CHECK**

Before your next interview, ask yourself:

- What's one truth I've been avoiding explaining clearly?

  ______________________________

  ______________________

- How would I explain it calmly, without apology or blame?

  ______________________________

  ______________________

# 20

# Humility: The Unspoken Differentiator

The most admired CEOs are rarely the loudest voices in the boardroom. As outlined in *The Power of Humility* by P.V. Ramana Murthy and *Good to Great* by Jim Collins, one of the defining traits of successful CEOs is *humility*. They speak less and listen more, give credit before taking it, and remain composed in moments of chaos. Their influence doesn't stem from dominating discussions but from quietly empowering others while calmly steering the ship.

This is the essence of humility—not a lack of confidence, but the presence of self-awareness. In interviews, just like in leadership, humility stands out—not because it shouts, but because it resonates. It signals maturity, emotional intelligence, and the willingness to keep learning.

Humility is not about downplaying your achievements. It's about presenting them with poise. It's the ability to say, '*I contributed, I learned, and I'm still growing,*' rather than '*I did it all.*'

In environments where assertiveness is often mistaken for ability, humility is the quiet truth that leaves a lasting impact. The same principle applies in interviews.

When you enter an interview room, your achievements matter—but how you carry them matters more. Humility isn't about downplaying your success. It's about acknowledging your journey, your mentors and your learning curve, and knowing there's more to come.

**Why Humility Works in the Interview Arena**

Corporate interviews are not just assessments of skill. They are assessments of attitude. And interviewers—especially at senior levels—aren't looking for arrogance wrapped in articulation. They're looking for:

- Learnability over loudness
- Collaboration over competition
- Self-awareness over self-promotion

## HUMILITY SIGNALS STRENGTH, NOT WEAKNESS

There's a misconception that being humble means being unsure. It doesn't. In fact, the most confident candidates are often the most grounded.

Because they know:

- They don't need to brag. Their work speaks.
- They don't need to interrupt. They listen, process, respond.
- They don't fake answers. They admit what they don't know and offer to learn.

And that last trait? That's gold in the eyes of recruiters.

## The Cricketing Analogy: Rahul Dravid vs Flashy Celebrations

Think of Rahul Dravid. Dependable. Calm. Fiercely skilled. Yet never theatrical. He didn't need a six to prove he could play—he let consistency, composure and quiet leadership define him.

Now picture that in an interview context. Imagine you are asked:

'You have led several high-impact projects. What do you think makes you successful?'

A candidate obsessed with self-glory may say, '*Because I always take charge. I lead from the front. I make things happen.*'

A humble, strategic candidate might say:

'*I have been fortunate to work with strong teams. I have learned to create space for others to excel. I think my strength lies in listening well, acting decisively, and learning fast—even from setbacks.*'

Guess which one feels more leader-like?

## What Humility Sounds like in Interviews

Use language that reflects clarity without conceit. For example:

- Instead of: '*I turned around the entire department.*'
  Say: '*I played a role in stabilizing the team during a difficult phase. It was a collective effort, and I learned a lot about managing transitions.*'
- Instead of: '*I knew exactly what to do.*'
  Say: '*I had some ideas based on prior experience, but I took time to understand the context before proposing a solution.*'

- Instead of: '*I am the best at what I do.*'
  Say: '*I have built deep expertise in this area, but I also keep updating myself—there's always more to learn.*'

Such responses don't dilute your strengths—they elevate your credibility.

**Practising Humility: A Few Ground Rules**

1. ***Credit Others Where Due***
   Mention mentors, team members or seniors who helped shape your journey. It shows gratitude and collaborative spirit.
2. ***Don't Pretend to Know Everything***
   Acknowledge knowledge gaps. Say, '*I haven't worked directly on this, but I would love to explore it further.*' It reflects confidence without conceit.
3. ***Speak Less. Listen More***
   Don't rush to impress. Reflect before you answer. The maturity in your pause speaks volumes.
4. ***Accept Feedback Gracefully***
   If an interviewer challenges a response, don't get defensive. Say, '*That's a useful perspective—I hadn't thought of it that way.*'
5. ***Avoid Over-Branding Yourself***
   You are not a product. You are a professional with a story. Don't oversell. Tell your story with clarity and let your experience breathe.

## FINAL THOUGHTS: WALK IN LIKE YOU BELONG, NOT LIKE YOU OWN THE ROOM

Humility is not timidity. It's the art of showing up with capability, curiosity and character. In a world where everyone wants to be seen, humility is your secret differentiator—it makes you memorable for all the right reasons.

Because at the end of the day, companies don't just hire the best talker. They hire the one who can listen, learn and lead, while lifting others up as well.

So, when you walk into your next interview, let your calm presence, thoughtful answers and self-assured humility win the game.

You don't need to raise your bat. Just keep hitting the right shots.

## Part C

---

# AFTER THE INTERVIEW: REFLECT, IMPROVE AND RISE

# 21

# Not Every Day Is a Century: Turning Rejections into Opportunities

Interviews are not just transactional conversations. They provide a foundation for discovery, introspection and growth. More than tests of knowledge, they measure your adaptability, resilience and emotional readiness for the challenges ahead.

In your journey, one truth becomes clear: Not every day is your day. Even the greatest falter. Sachin Tendulkar, arguably the finest to ever play the game, walked back for a duck many times. Yet, what made him extraordinary were not his centuries but his comebacks. Each failure only sharpened his resolve. The same holds true for interviews. They are not just about landing a job. They are about learning, evolving and staying the course.

## THE NATURE OF SETBACKS

Rejections sting. You wait for that call, that congratulatory email—instead, you receive a polite, templated regret. It feels personal. Sometimes, there's not even that. Just silence from the other end. You thought you did well, but there is no communication from the other side. It happens and is more common than you think. But it isn't a verdict on your worth. Sometimes, the alignment wasn't right. Maybe the panel had a different expectation. Maybe you missed a cue. Or maybe it just wasn't your day.

Just like Tendulkar didn't score a century every time he walked in, you won't crack every interview—and that's not failure. That's form. And form can always return.

## TRACK EVERY INTERVIEW LIKE A MATCH

Every interview you attend is a valuable data point in your career. Keep a record—not to dwell on failure, but to build insight.

Maintain a simple journal:

- Questions asked
- Your responses
- Panel dynamics and reactions
- What worked well; what didn't
- Any feedback received

Over time, these notes become your personal playbook—like a batsman watching tapes of his dismissals. Reflection leads to refinement. You will begin to notice patterns—phrases that land well, skills that keep getting tested, and reactions that reveal what truly matters. This awareness is how good candidates become great ones.

## WHY PERSEVERANCE IS EVERYTHING

Interviews test more than your resume—they test your character. Repeated rejections can dent confidence, but the key lies in your response. Do you give up—gear up!

Here's a story that puts this into perspective.

### The 12th Fail Who Refused to Quit

Manoj Kumar Sharma, now an IPS officer, failed his Class 12 exams and came from a background where just surviving was a daily struggle. But he had a dream—to join the civil services.

He didn't clear UPSC in his first attempt. Or his second. Or his third.

While working odd jobs to fund his studies—driving a tempo, working as a library assistant—he kept showing up, learning from each failure. He improved his communication, read newspapers aloud to sharpen articulation, and practised mock interviews in borrowed clothes.

On his *fourth attempt*, he cracked it.

What changed? Not the exam. Not the competition. Just his mindset and his refusal to give up.

Today, he says, '*Failures taught me more than success ever could.*'

His story is proof: You don't need to win every time—you just need to stay in the game one round longer than failure.

### The Battle-Hardened Mindset

Each interview adds something to your armour. What feels like failure today may be laying the foundation for your eventual breakthrough.

Ask yourself after every setback:

- Did I understand the industry or role better?
- Did I identify a gap I need to work on?
- Did I become more comfortable navigating tough conversations?

If even one answer is '*yes*', then the interview added value. And value compounds over time.

**Reframing Rejection**

Rejection only diminishes you if you let it. Instead, learn to reframe it.

Think of Tendulkar walking back after a first-ball duck. He didn't retreat—he reflected. He went back to the nets, recalibrated, and returned stronger. You should do the same.

Don't see rejection as a failure to impress. See it as feedback—often unspoken—that pushes you toward refinement.

Every 'no' is actually a 'not yet'. That shift in mindset can carry you through the darkest moments.

**Celebrate the Small Wins**

Success isn't always binary. Every interview holds mini-victories:

- Did you feel more confident this time?
- Did you answer that tricky question with better composure?
- Did you receive even one line of positive feedback?

These are not trivial. They are signs of growth. Track them. Celebrate them. Let them fuel you forward.

Progress is often invisible—until it becomes undeniable.

### The Uncertainty Is the Opportunity

No two interviews are the same. That's what makes them both daunting and full of possibility. Embrace this unpredictability. Each conversation, whether it ends in success or rejection, brings you closer to your goal.

Tendulkar's journey was filled with ebbs and flows. He wasn't defined by the ducks but by his determination to return, refine and rise.

So must you.

## FINAL TAKEAWAY: BUILD YOUR INNINGS WITH GRIT

Not every day will bring a hundred. But every day brings a chance to play, to learn and to prepare for the next innings.

Your job is to keep showing up.

- Keep applying
- Keep preparing
- Keep evolving

Because one day, all those 'nos' will fade—and a single 'yes' will rewrite your journey.

And when that day comes, you'll realize that the rejections weren't roadblocks—they were run-ups.

So, walk into every interview with the quiet confidence of a seasoned player. The job may not always come, but the growth will. And eventually, so will the century.

# 22

# Never Give up: Hope and Perseverance Lead the Way

There are phases in life that test not just your patience but your very sense of direction. Job hunting is one such phase—especially when met with repeated rejection or, worse, deafening silence. The wait for that one right opportunity can feel endless. But through it all, one word becomes your anchor—hope.

Even the most promising careers encounter moments of pause. Despite sincere effort, the calls don't come, or the interviews don't convert. It's frustrating, even demoralizing. But here's the truth: This is not your failure—it's a phase. And it's a shared human experience. Many accomplished professionals have walked this difficult path and emerged stronger.

**Strategy over Despair**

When the going gets tough, don't just keep moving—pause and pivot.

Start with your resume—the first window to your potential. Ask yourself:

- Is it tailored to the roles I am targeting?

- Does it highlight measurable achievements and current skills?
- Is it still reflecting the version of me from two years ago?

Many of us evolve professionally but forget to let our resume evolve with us. Keep it dynamic and ready. Even when not actively applying, make regular updates a habit. Opportunity doesn't knock—it searches.

Beyond the resume, evaluate your job-hunting strategy. Are you limiting yourself to one or two platforms? Are your profiles active and discoverable? In today's digital landscape, passivity is invisibility. Be visible. Be proactive.

## NETWORKING: YOUR HIDDEN ASSET

In moments of uncertainty, networking may seem intimidating—but that's exactly when it's most essential.

Begin with LinkedIn but don't stop there. Your outreach must be intentional and strategic, aligned with your domain and aspirations.

**How to Network with Purpose**

1. **Connect Intentionally:** Identify professionals in your field. Study their posts, learn from their journeys.
2. **Stay Visible:** Engage in discussions. Share insights. Let your professional identity shine through.
3. **Seek Guidance:** Send genuine messages—appreciate someone's work, ask for their perspective.
4. **Ask for Help** (Yes, Even Jobs)**:** It's okay to ask. But do it politely, with context and humility.

Here's the reality: you will face rejection. Or worse—silence. Most people won't respond. Some may say 'will connect later' and never do. But you only need a few to reply.

I remember a phase where I had to act on war footing. I sent hundreds of messages through personal LinkedIn windows. Most ignored them. Despite receiving no response in most cases, I didn't stop. I kept trudging forward—sludging through rejections, identifying new people to approach, and sending messages relentlessly. Eventually, two people responded positively, and both led to job offers. I didn't end up joining either, as I received another offer that was a better fit. But that's not the point. The point is—my consistent effort delivered results. It reaffirmed that perseverance, even in the face of silence, pays off. Every message I sent, every follow-up I did, brought me one step closer to the breakthrough I was looking for.

**Lean on Your People**

Job hunting may feel like a solitary journey, but it doesn't have to be walked alone.

Reach out to those who know you—friends, family, mentors and former colleagues. Not every conversation will lead to an opportunity, but some will lead to something far more valuable: renewed clarity, emotional strength and unexpected guidance.

Sometimes, it's a former teammate who refers you for a role. Sometimes, it's a mentor who reminds you of your worth when you're starting to forget it. Even a simple 'keep going, you are doing your best' can act as fuel when motivation runs low.

Support isn't always about solutions—it's about not feeling invisible during the struggle. Stay connected. Share your intent. And allow others the chance to help—many will, if only you ask.

**Stay in the Game: Update Job Portals Regularly**

Many assume that uploading a resume once on a job portal is enough. It isn't.

Most platforms prioritize recent activity. So, if your profile looks static, it drops in visibility. Make it a weekly or even daily habit to refresh your profile—update your summary, skills or keywords. Treat it like a living document. Recruiters notice activity—and seriousness.

**Engage beyond LinkedIn: Consultants and Circles**

Don't restrict yourself to digital networking. Engage with recruitment consultants. They may not always bring good news, but they are often plugged into market movements and roles that don't get advertised.

Build relationships even when they don't have an opening for you. Consultants remember persistence.

Similarly, speak to peers in your industry. Sometimes, a casual conversation over coffee leads to the breakthrough you were waiting for. Even if 90 per cent of your efforts lead nowhere, the remaining 10 per cent can change everything.

Activate every tool in your arsenal—from job boards to WhatsApp groups, alumni forums to internal referrals.

## WHEN HOPE FEELS HARD, HOLD ON HARDER

In the early days of my career, there were no job portals or professional networking sites—just the newspaper classifieds. I would diligently scan the listings, apply to roles that matched my profile, and then wait—often for weeks—without any response. But I didn't stop. I made it a routine, a discipline.

During that time, my mother underwent a critical surgery and slipped into a coma. It was one of the most emotionally devastating periods of my life. Yet, even while spending days in the hospital, I continued applying. One of the applications I sent during those difficult hospital visits led to a call. I was interviewed, and I got the job.

That role became the launchpad for my career. It didn't happen by chance—it happened because I refused to give up. Even in the darkest moments, persistence can lead to unexpected breakthroughs.

### The Story of Colonel Sanders

Here's a story you probably know.

Colonel Harland Sanders, the founder of KFC, didn't succeed until he was in his sixties. After retiring from a service station job, he cooked fried chicken using a unique recipe and went door to door to sell it to restaurants.

He was rejected 1,009 times.

Yes—*1,009 rejections.*

But he kept going.

Eventually, someone gave him a chance. Today, his face is on one of the most iconic global food brands. His story isn't about chicken. It's about grit. It's a reminder: You don't need everyone to say yes—you just need one.

## CLOSING THOUGHTS: THE POWER OF QUIET PERSISTENCE

Hope is not passive. It's not wishful thinking. It's a decision—to show up, every day, even when the results aren't there yet.

Remember:

- Keep sending those resumes.
- Keep refining your strategy.
- Keep reaching out.
- Keep going.

You don't need a hundred green lights—just one.

And when it comes, it won't just change your job—it will change your life.

# 23

# Your Interview Journey: From Preparation to Triumph

As we bring this journey to a close, let's reflect on a powerful truth: Interviews are not just a stepping stone to your next job—they are a transformative experience that can shape your professional identity. They challenge you to articulate your aspirations, highlight your achievements, and navigate uncertainties with confidence. With the insights and strategies shared throughout this book, you now hold the tools to not only excel in interviews but to approach them as opportunities for growth and self-discovery.

## KILLER INSTINCT: THE MINDSET THAT WINS INTERVIEWS

To succeed in interviews, you need killer instinct—the inner belief that '*I can do it*', backed by hard work and intelligent preparation. It's the mindset that pushes you to not just show up, but to stand out. It fuels you to go the extra mile, to stay calm under pressure, and to finish strong when it matters most.

Take Sourav Ganguly, for instance. When he took over as captain, Indian cricket was at a crossroads—timid abroad, low on confidence. But with his fierce determination and refusal to settle for mediocrity, Ganguly infused his team with belief. He built a unit that fought back, played with intent, and never feared failure. That's killer instinct—not aggression, but clarity, courage and conviction.

In interviews, that's what sets you apart. Not just knowing answers, but showing intent. Not just speaking well, but making them believe you are the one. You will not stop till the goal is reached and yes, a little Ganguly-like grit.

## THE FINAL WORDS

As you step into your next interview, carry this thought with you: You have everything it takes to succeed. The skills you have developed, the experiences you have gathered, and the insights you have gained have all prepared you to seize the opportunity ahead.

Approach each interview with curiosity, confidence and clarity. View every question as a chance to share your story, and every challenge as a moment to shine. You are not just seeking a job; you are crafting a career—building a legacy of growth, impact and purpose.

The corporate world is vast and full of possibilities. With the strategies in this book—and the belief that you belong—you are ready to navigate its challenges, embrace its opportunities, and thrive on your terms.

The preparation is done. The field is set. Now go and win the match.

Here's to your success and the incredible journey ahead. Go forth and conquer!

# A Note from the Author

If this book helped you see interviews not as a test but as an opportunity to express your story—then it has served its purpose.

But let me also say this: This book is not just theory—it is a product of lived experience. Every chapter, every insight and every strategy shared here comes from real conversations, real rejections, real breakthroughs. I have seen what works, what fails, and what transforms an average candidate into a memorable one.

These pages reflect years of learning—often the hard way. And that is why, if you follow the path laid out here with diligence, reflection and honest effort, it will not just prepare you for interviews—it will equip you to clinch the prized role you aspire for.

So, carry forward the mindset, apply the methods, and trust the process.

You are closer than you think.

**The Finish Line Is Just the Starting Point**

Completing this book is not the end of your preparation—it's the beginning of your execution. What lies ahead is not just a series of interviews but opportunities to define your future. With focus, resilience and intent, you now have everything you need to turn potential into performance. Stay hungry. Stay ready. Your moment is waiting.

# Before Your Next Interview

Before you step into the room—physical or virtual—pause.

Not to revise answers.

Not to memorize lines.

But to centre yourself.

Ask yourself, quietly and honestly: Do I know why I am here—why this role, why this organization, why now?

Not the safe answer. The true one.

Can I explain my journey—including the detours—without defensiveness, apology or exaggeration?

Not as a justification, but as a narrative of learning and choice.

Do my stories reflect judgement and impact, not just effort and activity?

If asked 'So what?' would my answers hold?

Am I prepared to listen, not just respond?

To engage, not perform?

Do I trust—deeply—that I belong in the room I am about to walk into?

Not because I am perfect, but because I am prepared, reflective and still growing.

If you can sit with these questions calmly, the interview changes shape.

It is no longer a test to clear.

It becomes a conversation to enter.

A decision to explore—on both sides.

Close this book knowing this:

You don't need to impress everyone.
You need to be clear, honest, and present.
That is what carries through pressure.
That is what gets remembered.

Now step in.
The next innings is yours.

# In Gratitude

To everyone who interviewed me—you helped me grow.

To everyone I have had the chance to interview—you helped me reflect.

Each exchange has shaped my journey in more ways than I can express.

To my parents, for their blessings; and to my dear wife, Jayati, and son, Dwaipayan—thank you for your belief and constant encouragement.

And to the editorial team at Rupa, especially Mr Dibakar Ghosh and Ms Anupama Roy, your insights, clarity and suggestions made this book sharper, stronger and more meaningful.